Someone

Will Go On

Owing

Someone

Will Go On

Owing

Selected Poems: 1966–1992

ANDREW GLAZE

Black Belt Press

Montgomery

The Black Belt Press

P.O. Box 551

Montgomery, AL 36101

Library of Congress Cataloging-in-Publication Data

Glaze, Andrew.
    Someone will go on owing / Andrew Glaze.
        p. cm.
      ISBN 1-881320-91-X (hardcover)
      ISBN 1-881320-93-6 (softcover)
    I. Title.
    PS3557.L38S66 1997
    811'.54—dc21   97-16915
                                                              CIP

Design by Randall Williams
Printed in the United States of America
98 99 00   5 4 3 2 1

*The Black Belt, defined by its dark, rich soil, stretches across central
Alabama. It was the heart of the cotton belt. It was and is a place of
great beauty, of extreme wealth and grinding poverty, of pain and joy.
Here we take our stand, listening to the past, looking to the future.*

Gratefully as ever,

to Ted Haddin and Steven Ford Brown,

without whom this book would not have been possible.

Contents

Someone Will Go On Owing

When I'm gone to that principality of sleep
of which I'm the warring field,
my daddy parts the seething veil
to whisper we must work
to make the world go right.

Then mama warns me, and warns me in the obverse
"Be watchful of desperate good intent.
Nothing born, no matter how it tries,
is more than halfway true."

So I undream, perplexed, the grisly rights and wrongs,
the million good-hearted ways
which spring up like dragon's teeth from the tilth
in which I've long since sowed an earnest faith
that I can love irreconcilables into one,
and track my pettifoggeries and crimes
back to their human birth in goodwill.

Someone will go on owing.
Such is the nature of life.
But to whom?
And how is such a hopeless
abandonment ever to be paid off?

from *Reality Street,* 1991

Introduction

By PABLO MEDINA

Imagine a gaunt man standing alone in a park of our city blurting out words. He has funny ears and bent eyeglasses. He appears to be speaking to no one in particular: "Stop kissing essences, Learn to respect / your essential rumpy importance." You wave him off, continue eating your lunch sandwich. "Sin is being forced to notice / what you're thinking about all the time anyway." You take another bite. ". . . God was the first institution in our city . . ." You chew. "Ail! ail! for I am the Waltz of the Garbage / whose battalions of sign bearers / beat their plaques into butterfly wings . . ." You realize that this man is a poet, not an unusual discovery in New York, where it appears that every other person has published a chapbook; but this particular poet can sing his language, like the great ones:

> Was it with Grandpa or Robert Frost
> I rode out to look for the way we lost?
> I remember one had a beard, and one did not—
> but which one?
> One spoke with a stutter of gold,
> and one had an aim—
> which one?
> —and one had a guilt,
> and where has that single tree gone
> I remember they said they built?
>
>   ("Tick Tock")

Within the music is sense, well-wrought and well-earned. You put down your sandwich, forget about eating, and listen to whole poems as they come: "Glory," "I Come in Late," "Grandpa," "The People of My Head," "Reality Street," "Fantasy Street," "Inventory," "Coo Coo," "Melt Out." You decide not to go back to work. The sun goes down. You fall asleep to the poet's words.

I first met Andrew Glaze in Miami, two weeks after Hurricane Andrew all but destroyed the city. I had moved to Miami in search of who-knows-what and found myself literally in the vortex of one of the worst storms of the century. With me I had a few names and phone numbers, among them Andrew Glaze's, which was given to me by Martin Mitchell, the editor of *Pivot,* a magazine that has consistently published some of Glaze's best recent work. As soon as phone service was restored, I called Andrew Glaze. With a grace and good manners that, I later learned, run deep in his blood, he greeted me and suggested we have lunch together a few days later at La Carreta, a Cuban restaurant on Calle 8, in the heart of Little Havana. He was happy to hear from someone from up North, especially a poet.

Glaze looked so out of place in La Carreta that he seemed actually to fit somehow, as if he had been placed there to make everyone else feel at home. He was slim and athletic-looking and carried himself with a fluidity and economy of movement surprising for someone in his seventies. Later I found out he practiced yoga and ballet (see his poem "Nijinski") and played golf at least once a week. I ordered soup, caldo gallego, I think; he had something much heavier, which would have put me into a deep slumber for the rest of the afternoon. He bemoaned the fact that he was taking medication which prevented him from drinking. We talked about the hurricane, the major topic of conversation there those days; we talked about his dislike of Miami, how he would rather be in New York, where he thought he had always belonged; and we talked about poetry, his, mine, others'. On parting, he gave me one of his books.

We spoke again the following week. "Call me Andy," he said. "I don't want to be associated in any way with that horrible storm." We met, this time at his house and I brought him my book; he gave me another of his, which I promptly read that night, by candlelight, for electricity had not yet been restored to our part of the city. Over the next few months I read more of Glaze's work and discovered a great range of subject matter, as well as a singularity of voice and vision. Within this vision is a calm acceptance of displacement as a basic element of the human condition. Look at poems like "My South," "George Washington's Mud," "Earl," and "Laughter." Counterbalancing the displacement is an involvement with the texture of everyday life. His anchors are not abstractions but the objects around him that he can see and touch and hear: "Reality is something like me carrying / the bicycle down the steps in the morning, / with a grip at the seat socket on the left / and the stem of the steering post on the right . . ." ("Reality Street"). How intolerant Glaze is of anything—aesthetic posturing, intellectual hubris—that takes him away from quotidian existence; how nakedly he pronounces against the status quo, aeshetic, political, and social, and how powerful (because they are naked) his pronouncements are. "Poetry had better be shocking or shut up," he says in "A Letter to David Matzke." "What earthly good to say / that Spring will be around again next year?"

It is natural then to hear Whitman, Frost, and Williams lurking in these poems. Additionally, there is a simplicity of attitude in Glaze's work that will not tolerate foolishness. But do not be fooled by that simplicity. Underneath it lies a complexity of thought and syntax not always present in the above-mentioned triad of poets but more usually associated with Gerald Manley Hopkins, with Osip Mandelstam and César Vallejo, both of whom Glaze has masterfully translated, and with Emily Dickinson, to whom Glaze will go on owing as long as he writes poetry. I point you to poems like "Grandpa," "Inventory," "Cats Cradle," and the wonderfully playful (but dead serious) "Coo Coo."

Because of his originality and because of his reluctance to be fashionable for the sake of currying favor, this poet has had to stand alone, not alienated exactly, but away from the bright lights and the big stage, lurking at the edges, hiding in the corners where true art is always made. That position has provided him an Erasmian perch from which to observe human folly (his own as well as others'), understand it, and, finally, celebrate it. Take a look at the wonderful paean to individualism titled "Earl," at "The Fanatical You," a poem which unabashedly celebrates the demonic, and at "The Don Quixote of the Kitchen Table," which ends, "Who sinks his spurs in facts / is already lost," a poetic statement Cervantes himself would admire.

Yes, Glaze stood alone for the many years he has been a poet, refusing to write the precious gilded pieces that clutter too many literary magazines. That apartness has not been without its frustration, but it has accorded him an unflinching eye, clear and sharp and true. It has also allowed him to understand that while poetry is for everyone, it is not for the masses. It is neither solution nor garland, neither prophecy nor propaganda, but a way, a means. It is a life:

> But there's no guidebook to this country.
> Fly-specks and bird-droppings
> have been mistaken for the map.
> Where is the arsenal hiding, where it's made?
>
> ("Sweepings")

You awake in the park just as the sun is coming up. The birds are singing. The poet is nowhere to be found. You feel as if you had drunk a great deal of wine the night before, and there are poems and fragments of poems floating in and out of your consciousness—"Here we are taking a ride / in the buggy . . . / Old Starlight chop-chops, / hindquarters stretching like chewing, / in my face." You remember those lines from "Grandpa." And you remember this from "Make Room": "I want to finish redecorating/be able to ask Death into my house, / show him the chairs, / the table I made myself, / crack him a walnut / (give him the good part) / introduce him to my children, / offer him a drink . . ."

You look around, realize you want to drink more of this heady stuff, these winedark poems; but the man has disappeared. Then you glance down at the park bench where you have been sleeping and see next to you a manuscript wrapped with shoestring—a gift from a place where we all live and where anything is possible. It is titled *Someone Will Go On Owing,* by A. G.

Someone

Will Go On

Owing

Damned Ugly Children

1963

Damned Ugly Children

My poems, you are damned ugly children.
I love every one of you anyway—
your scabby hook noses, wall eyes, and crab feet.
I could swear I didn't make you for their judgment,
and I'd only half lie.
I mean what do I care what they say?
And it's true—somehow I never thought of us
as having business with their war of traffic.

We were being most ourselves,
I was making you for someone to talk to.
—Someone to stare with through that dirty window
out in the courtyard where the impossible squats
dressed in long rainbow-colored questions.
She was the only prophet I ever thought much of.

And because I made you against every possibility,
we shall never give up our old secrets, god knows.
Didn't I get you out of the iron claws
of my own possessive guts
to give to myself for a birthday present?

Goodbye Captain Rickenbacker

Goodbye to the airplane,
to the fabulous ailerons,
to the honest wheels
as large as pearl buttons
rolling in grass,
and the pistons of castor oil
and the sleek heads of the scarf-sailing pilots,
chewing wads in the prop-waste.
They leap off up black crag stairs of clouds
to spool down darkness like thread.

Goodbye to the aerodromes,
with the windsocks cocked like plump fingers,
booming with metal hammers and cheesecloth staplers.
Goodbye to the radios
heaped in static, popping like operations.
Goodbye to the long-tire-black tarmac
sweeping like rain down endless scalding cups
of earliest fresh morning coffee.

The Erl Child

I've always voted in elections,
I've been a good democrat all my life.
I am coterminous with everybody, and everybody
is a piece of me. But there is something
in me that doesn't vote.
In the morning it tells me when I walk down to the village
where they give me bad eggs, bad bacon,
bad looks, and a bad reputation,
that this is not where I was born.
There was some perfidious star,
there was flaming at the coffee ring
and white-coated waiters walking about in the dark.
A tall white lady was putting Scottish socks on my feet,
arranging around my head
a silk blanket and jade jacket-fastenings.
I remember being carried down by rushes and a stream.
I keep looking in the attic for a basket.
Someday I shall turn over an old sewing machine
or broken hamper and there it will have been all the time.
I'll open it and find the wristlet,
the enamels, the identification ring, the money,
and (I hope with an intact seal)
the morocco box with the tape and the stamp inside
and the book of the code.

Earl

He was twenty. He was sincerely crazy.
With his head like a half-baffled chocolate Easter egg,
there he was painting my house in Birmingham, Alabama,
doing things backwards,
painting from the bottom up
so the new paint from above
ran down on the new paint below,
putting turpentine in the watercolors.
He always jumped from the back porch roof
to the ground—fourteen feet.
—I used to be a paratrooper, said Earl—
I came down in the war with Russia
shooting a submachine gun around me in circles,
nobody had a chance to get a bead on me—
I shot them first. They thought
I was the holy, iron-assed, frosted bird.
I won the war—

The top of the house was fifty feet in the air,
The ladder was forty.
Earl fastened the ladder to the gutter.
He nailed a two by four with wooden cleats
to the top of the ladder.
He nailed a paintbrush to the broom.
He climbed and sat up on the top of them all.
He looked like a man just out of a fountain spray
of white paint. He waved the paintbrush
over his head like a banner on top of the broom.
He yelled out over the roofs of Birmingham, Alabama,
—look at me up here—
Look at me! Anybody want to argue?—

A Letter to David Matzke

The beautiful is always bizarre—Baudelaire

I tell you, David,
poetry ought to be shocking,
and poets ought to be dangerous people.
In whatever country, honest feeling is always
      shocking and dangerous,
and anyone true to the heart can simply enough and at
      any time be both.

But for their contempt we've ourselves to blame.
We've been cowardly, making the stuff so cheap
begging their love
that poets are poor people
from wearing out the money of never was
passing it back and forth among themselves.

Rub the truth in their faces!
What is the point of being a poet anyway,
if you can't be a kind of prophet?
Hold their nose to the stink,
say "Look, this is it!
We are here by ourselves,"
say "There's no kind uncle,
you will have to furnish the kindnesses out of your
      own pocket.
If you see that, nothing can hurt you!
Stop kissing essences. Learn to respect
your essential rumpy importance.
And for God's sake, don't mistake my words for food,
when they're nothing but spoons."

Say with whatever gestures are customarily indecent
and the wildest possible musical accompaniment
"The sky will not move
for buckets of moonlight and French quotations."
While they're watching you chant like a demon priest,
(some of us love these pitiful games)
kick away all those roses covering the cesspool.
How else make clear
that if there's a reason
we bawl these songs to ourselves
as we push this stone to nowhere
for no apparent reason,
the reason's only too simple to be believed—
like the snake swallowing his tail.

That music is useless—
and by that token as great as the universe.
This alone, if they could understand it,
would overturn all their systems.

Shout something simple and sensible.
For instance, that nothing done in boredom
is a human accomplishment.
They'll think you're talking about leisure
or the family cookout. Make it clear you're not.
Don't worry. If you brandish it either seriously or humorously
and go ahead and shout it in the street,
they'll only mistake you for a deluded
arsonist or communist.

But remember, they will smell out the truth
            behind their fear
and roll you in the garbage to comfort their taught lies.
So, you must understand them.

They've only this one poor fence against accepting the nature
        of themselves
and they truly fear it.
They'll never suspect you're a poet,
poetry has no importance,
and they can't allow you a worthwhile reason to deserve
        to be whipped.
Take comfort that you're being punished for the wrong reason.

When you speak of love,
they'll try to pretend you mean Cleopatra
or some other anal-vaginal queen.
Only two or three will recognize your corrosive subversity,
They're your audience.
Make sure the others have to twist themselves into idiots
to misunderstand the difference.

Are you afraid?
If not, there's something wrong with you!
To tell them what they care for most
is as relevant to their lives
as the sugar level of the urine of pregnant beetles?
But you ought to be afraid of dying without having tried!
Make them call out the cops if possible.
Poetry had better be shocking or shut up.
What earthly good to say
that Spring will be around again next year?

Missionary

I shall never fit in, I've promised it to myself.
If it were not for being different,
what would I have to proud of?
My best grades in school were in being unlike anybody.

Therefore I must take sleeping pills to sleep,
eating pills to eat,
breathing pills to breathe, sense of humor pills to laugh,
in the happy pretense of making life happen.

Of course, this way, the poet I feel most at home with is Mayakowsky,
who blew out his brains.
But I learn from him never to do that—
that he should have had balance,
and balanced on into the red dawn dancing.
My dawn is orange, and my dance
the Baldwin County Apple Jug.

You see, I'm safe, and always consult the proper institutions
so I may overturn along the way what is not human.
I stamp it until it is dead, and burn it with kerosene.
That way I remain incurably naive. I made up my mind
when I was fifteen years old, to be forever fifteen,
and I refuse to notice any of the reasons to change my mind.
I train myself to look away from signs of smallness
because I believe in the grandeur of the Human Race.

But there are disadvantages. You have to join the crowd to make
        money,
and I'm bored with poverty. I don't at all enjoy
being unsuccessful, as I ought, despite long serious talks

with my conscience, which keeps
looking in the dark like Whistler's mother.

And I worry what should be my aim.
Someone suggested I go to Cambodia
and be a missionary to the Khmers. I'd teach them to be good
and they'd teach me great art.
But then I learn they have disappeared
more than five hundred years.

That's the sort of problem I'm always stumbling on.
But it's better anyway—keeping busy—
better than thinking about this crazy era
where like all the other crazy eras
insane custom is still busy being king.
If I let myself grow up and join in, I will start to bother them,
to shout "Where are you going, uncle Everybody,
are you insane?" I will run out in the street and shout
"Where are you off to now, with that horrible pistol
of the ego in your coat pocket!"
So at last they'd notice me. That I'm different.
And I hate to think about that.

Tall Talk

I hated my Anglo-Saxon heart.
It was so anxiously upright,
in this city of myself the mayor and aldermen were so fierce,
so determined to brick me up for rectitude
that I didn't think I could ever learn to be true.
My plazas were closed, my cafes stank of talk,
I couldn't by any ingenuity of wishing or forcing
open my gates to trade with any beast or tree.

I thought of calling out the mobs to riot in my dreams.
I'd shake my fist in my imagination's face
and pile up the paving stones
and shout "dirty old politicians!"
I'd give up my beaux arts and roll my name in the dirt.
I was sick of declaiming the lines of that same legal script,
sick of the mock-serious veins of judicial blood—
but how do you rub a government off your face?

And all the time my heart was so wiseacre smug, so civicly sure
going on its accustomed nepotistic way,
not in the least minding all the tall talk,
oh it was willing for me to sit and talk tall-talk all day.
Why do they always forget
that when you have been shut up enough
you will burn it all down including yourself in the risk?

I did. I set the fire. Lit the flame in my eye,
—bang went aldermen, courthouse, cafes, and gates,
spinning over and over up high and coming down
in a wreckage of lintels and bonbons and pride.

The horizon bobbled and stung with the debris.
So without really believing it could happen,
I found myself sitting on the ground—
free! free!

I looked up at the wildly empty sky.
It was like a newborn unfamiliar dream.
For the first time in my life, I had neither shield nor friend,
no place, no enemy, no time.
I crouched there counting the holes in my pockets.
The wind was cold, there was no wall nor roof
nor any fire to keep me warm.
I began to dance.

Black Angels

Four or five times a year they come to see me,
pressing their dried-bean ghost faces
against my kitchen window.
They stare angrily at me. I know who they are—
they are those who against all reason fought
before me the mad-dog of everyday in the name of the heart.

They glare at my new yellow kitchen
and white icebox.
Their desiccated saw-grass rustling voices
whisper "we walked out of their camp
in bitter rags—
we starved, we gave, we died,
that something should at least appear to matter,
even if only in that brief shriek
of that poor cut-off thing—that we care.
Brother, haven't you taken their bribe, their bribe,
                              their bribe?"

At first, I thought, if I throw these people
the rinds of my true misery
they'll know I'm one of them all along, and go away.
But no—they paw over and sniff the wretched trash—
as though assaying it for something I can't guess—
and then come and scratch at my window again.
Still, in a strange way I feel they are my friends.
To prove it one of them once put out a fingernail
and laid upon my windowsill
A single green and moldy tear.

But somehow to me the world they seem to see as a battle
                    is really a show.
And I put on my green silk tights and practice the act
in which I swear I will force my way
through the hoop of fire of the living barricade
and over the blind acrobats on the tumbling floor.

And whacking myself on the back and shouting
"It doesn't matter! It doesn't matter!" like the family battle cry,
while everybody shrieks in amazement to see me
                    fling myself so,
I try again and again to be caught in the act.
I throw my body by sheer brute force
through the flaming air, aiming with fat squat wings
at the fact set just underneath the great blue tent mouth
                    hung by the door.

—Sometimes I almost make it. I touch fingertips—
and then, broken-backed, flop every time
                    in the sawdust pit
and lie there shocked and out of breath.
And it's there—each time,
when I've made a fool of myself once more
by thinking that all these impossible things could be done.
I expect them to fall down laughing. And they don't.
And I hate them even more for not having forced
                    their advantages.
Damned black angels!
Where did they get the right to judge my life?
What do they want? Oh, I know—I suspect they're waiting
until that one last time when I fall and can't get up
and can't laugh either.
Then they'll have me down unable to move
with a subdivided intention.

And knowing the way I can't give way and let
                    things happen,
they will kneel and take my helpless hand
as the acts go on and off and on
and—how will I be able to endure it!—
They'll commiserate with my final fury and despair.

The Glory

I had been twenty years fastening the glory onto the
                            front porch
when out the front door opens and here comes Alf.
—What are you doing there, lad—he hails me,
—Knock off work, the moratorium's declared,
—I ain't all finished,—I said—with this here glory,
it lacks a bit of the gold leaf on the foot of it
of bein' after the plan—now that don't matter—
                            he said,
—glories has been declared redundant too,
go home and gum your stick and have your year of pension.
But I wouldn't hear of that, I finished the glory
and watched them tear the head off it for scrap
with comfortable satisfaction, for hadn't I done
what they had paid me for and gave my sleep?
And if they didn't want a glory anymore,
well, hadn't I got the job of it to keep?

Zeppelin

Someone has built a dirigible in my parlor.
What on earth has happened to the boarders?
I go in there sometimes
and tear the fabric off the framework, I shout
"who's responsible for this?"
but nobody answers.
There's nothing underneath
but a wilderness of girders
and a gas bag without any gas.
The dog has taken to living in one of my shoes.
Poor thing! His blanket was by the fireplace,
now filled up with the underfin.
When the propellers turn they open the doors,
they scatter papers down the hall to the garden,
sometimes they blow the paper I'm reading into my face.
My first editions are soggy with crankcase oil,
and the batik shawl I brought from ancient Mesopotamia
is soaked in grease.
Up there the pointed cone upon the nose
protrudes through my Matisse.
The pilot (at least I suppose he's the pilot)
is balled up on my bed, and when I shake him
he lifts one flap of his aviator's tarboosh to shout
"I didn't do it" and something that sounds like
"metal fatigue." He burrows into my pillow
deeper with his head. I saw a man in a mechanic's uniform
climb up inside this morning. I said
"look here now, this is my living room!"
He only banged with his wrench,
shook his fist at my fractured plaster and shouted
"what's important is that in the end it fly!"

I have to admire his singleness of mind.
Why it isn't even a new model. "Gott straff England"
is written across the gondola with lipstick in gothic lettering.
One of these mornings I've got to get out and see my lawyer.
Maybe he will suggest somebody to sue.
In the meantime for my conscience' sake
I need someone authoritative to tell me
what are the principles involved,
I mean so I will know if I should
feel resentful or honored.

The Bigger-Better

Make it bigger—he said.
And my god, there I was flat on my back
in the downstairs darkness
chewing away at that papier mâché monument
already fifty feet high,
why it lost itself in the gloom up there by the rafters,
in the dark up there where nobody human could see it.

A quarter of a century, I thought,
making myself a present of this!
Plastering it all out of chewed hard rocks and curses
and a millon cups of coffee sweetened with spit!
—bigger!—I shouted—you bastard!
It's bigger already than Barnum and Bailey!
It's wished on me shin splints and peg calluses,
and look at how time is sitting on my knees like a secretary.
Look at me, Kleig Lights!
I have heaven's conundrum of grace deciphered,
what am I doing here screwed down in this mud?—
I said—keep your peace!

As soon as I finish this one damn thing I'll go.
I'll go outside and sit by the scullery door
and toast my knuckles at the coals of the sun
and let the vines inquire my address of the stones—
Well, there wasn't any answer but the drip of the leak
                              in the sink.
—And who are you—I said—to make a measurement.
I'm the master of my calluses!
I won't build anything bigger than it's fun—
—so I made it bigger.

Ice-Break

One Spring day I undid my door,
with a frigid snick of lock and key,
till it broke,
and I stood on the step of the sun
where I grew dizzy under an absolute sky,
and far Cathays of horizon
shouted from every scattering degree of the compass.

From up against the street's top,
the windy campaniles
of rookeries and clattering tiles,
came volleys of wingclaps,
the air-washed hosannahs of pigeons.
Winds made music out of the belfries of air.
I half forgot who I was, and came awake
to the last part,
fire to the sun, water to the sea,
tipped out across the air to wine.
It made my drink a molten thing
to tilt me so upon my ear
a prey to the coming together of chances.

But just when I had got it right,
it began to shrink,
time began to slide downhill
and shouts and rings and pennybright chances
coasted to sun on rocks and chinks
and strangely as I was rich and great
I stood empty-hearted and empty-handed
watching the soot-clerks sweeping the streets.

Cats

One night,
walking home from work
with my black brief case of stones
down 50th street,
just at dizzy-glittering dusk,
I thought I saw a yellow cat,
up high.

I stopped and blinked
and cats popped out in all colors
over the roofs and eaves,
across the fronts of old hotels,
at first by threes and fours,
then more and more,
crouching along the building tops
till all the lights were walking,
hopping across the ledges
in necklaces of curious-colored cats.

The reds were stretching
languorous paws, reaching me-ward
anxious to see if they could reach my eyes.
Up high the whites walked telegraph wires,
attenuating to poles and loops like rings of stars.
Blue cats fought, whizzing and skirling,
blinking a fuzz of frozen static code.
They sprang across the sky with saber claws.
There were green cats
rolling flying somersaults into the void.

And all at once they all began to run,
dragging the underneath about,
coasting the soft beige sidewalks off
to the left off underneath out from me,
a thousand rainbow-colored cats leapt off
and flew.
Then I said "scat!" and closed my eyes.

There was a moment's silence and the coldness
of a million unblinking yellow irises.

Something brushed like pads of fur
along the inside of my lid,
though my eyes were tightly closed,
I stood at the center of a bass-thumping
carousel of grinning yellow cats.
They ringed my neck like strings of frivolous beads.
I flew in a second on vowels of chaos and bottomless flight.
My briefcase whistled night and day like a reel.

So Many Separate Marvelous Persons

So many separate marvelous persons
Each a sun with planets and stars.
Don't you see
tomorrow is nothing compared with that?

And the sky bulging down
in the enormous way that just this minute chooses,
under a monk's hood of cloud—

I light a little flame.
My match scratches
like a powder train in a sea battle of the past.
Yesterday was a dead word the minute it was born.

Today is the sense of this minute,
an ocean out of sight of land.
The streets tower like blunt seas.
Climbing the mast of the moment like a powder monkey,
look out over the leagues.
Make out more than a dozen ships.

The Ball

Putting down flooring in the attic, I moved something
to one side and found the afternoon I was fourteen.
I turned it over and over in my hand and looked at it again.
It was the day I climbed the fire escape
and made myself a mechanical toy utopia
all by myself—
out of old radiators and worn out pine verandahs
lugged up there to keep them secret,
hidden away behind the smell of heirlooms
deep in the cache where my father never thought
to put his common sense to work and make that too, practical.

It hadn't changed. A system, still sealed up
in a skin-tight patent-leather jazz-ball, hard and bright.
It was maybe my last chance to try the thing.
I let it go. The way it whizzed up past the back-porch roof
my father would have thought it was the moon if he had seen it.
He could not have gotten it down.
Something that once begun rose up so fast and skimmed so lofty
I never could catch it again myself,
and if I had, so smooth I never could break it,
and if I had, so white-hot warm inside
it would blow up and fleck all over
dappling the race with flies of fire.

The Marriage

I waked up one morning in an unfamiliar double bed.
Where am I?—I said, and I replied
—married to art, that's where—I shrugged.
Well, purity had always been my monogram,
and this was a suitable match to the morally fortified,
it was about as adequate a false face

to put on as any, I supposed.

But just as I breathed out to put life in my bride,
something shut up in the cellar
went "knock! knock!"
I got out of bed. I didn't want to be interrupted.
I screwed down the door and piled on trash
trying not to guess what it was.
Then I hid because I began to realize
that whatever it was, it was against me.
I climbed up and burrowed down in the attic under wool,
my bride could retrieve her own good things and run,
because I was stuck there for a while,
and below far down I could hear the thongs fly off,
the nails gibber and groan.

And though I got busy and made door braces and collapsible
stairs,
carpentry, I was discovering, is no use when something rises.
And that vision was rising.
Vision? I didn't believe in visions!
But something was rising, I could hear it, couldn't I?
Breaking through the floor! I was finding my marriage

hidden behind that something like a tree
like Christmas morning rising covered with lights
more implacable even than a tree.
Red—blue—green—
now knocking! Don't tell me it wasn't there!
When I could see it!
Rapping on the clouds that weren't there either,
one—two—three!

Adam

Ask the children with no fathers.
Did I kill their fathers?
Ask old men who rise at 4 a.m.
to curse each other in their spit.
Ask old ladies stomping each other's toes—
calling each other cow,
did I make them do it?

Damned nagging values! What do they want for a bribe?
Did I ask to be wildly and happily born in luck?
Did I ask to be born to be justified?
Did I ask to be made responsible for this—and this?

I didn't. I deserve it anyway.
There's a frivolous hangman in me
wants work.
He hangs me here with this harsh prong in my heart
on my own hook.

My South

I

Before me, it was grandpa's old mad South,
the funhouse of principle.
A sort of Baptist revival in a whorehouse,
with violent rapes in the purities,
and John Locke snatching up the souls
and boiling them down into Presbyterian whisky.

We were so alone with our familyness—
(Grandma standing by the cistern threatening to jump in)
and a deep, still, limestone-well of love and service in our dream.
(Grandpa letting out all his money
in personal notes
because he believed in gentlemanliness—
raising a houseful of children
without speaking to his wife.)
We were incessantly and purposely pursuing
any policy that hid our fundamental nature from us.
(Sin is being forced to notice
what you're thinking about all the time anyway).

What we saw most clearly
wasn't real at all.
In the name of some imaginary world
my Uncle Mike in Florida was shooting at the neighbors,
pursuing property rights like the true cross,
and Aunt Billie stayed at home in Tennessee
to mind the rats, the wind in the cracks,
the old books, the phonograph in the parlor,
her vision of them all, glorious and loving.

In its name she kept her mother alive
on chickenfood and vitamins.
She thought she was nourishing a saint.
Grandma, that old crafty intellectual pirate,
she knew what it was about. Simply one more way
of getting fall-down drunk on sentiment.

And in its name my father shot himself and his secretary.
Behaviorism and science
are not enough to save from the cannibal ego.

They wring their hands when none of the furious
                    dreams come true.
And not that anything fails to come about because of their
                    lack of zeal!
God! Effort is the lodestar of their lives.
Enlisted in an endless civil war against reality
of which each act is a prodigy of humorless sweat,
and wildly pursuing the bright stars of the Christmas sparklers,
laying hand on the hot metal—mistaking the agony for truth—
determined to think that what the senses know—is a dream—
and what is only dreamed—is the true flesh and bone.
They are eternally astounded when
the face of the torturer unmasks and is goodwill—
their own.

One day in Alabama when the Johnson grass by the rail yard
                    was green on the slag-pile,
one day in Birmingham, Alabama,
in an old green Plymouth, I was a witness.
A deputy of the sheriff's, dressed as neatly as a clerk,
knocked about in the street two dead-drunk colored men
who scraped the fender of their car on mine.
And when I testified what happened at the trial,

48   SOMEONE WILL GO ON OWING

and later they had sued him on his bond,
that man came down to my room with warm hurt eyes,
I swear he was a very gentle man, and said
"Now how you can do this to me I don't see,
to testify for two drunk niggers.
Don't you know I got a family?
I done it only as a favor to you,
I ask you now, what business was it of mine?
Me off duty taking my wife for a drive!—
I only got in it to help you, man—
ain't you got a religion?
Ain't you never heard of the Golden Rule?"

So once a day, with all these things in mind,
I take a handful of dirt, of skin,
and I say to myself, "Here, right here, this is the place."

Some families are born without fingers,
some people are born without senses. Which is sad.
But I think there is a much more terrible thing,
—to be reared without one's own consent
in the cave of the mind like a faded fish
and to go as assuredly blind in the soul as a saint.

          II

In this ugly foreign city where I've come to be
                    more or less at home,
to which I was shot upward
like a flaming lava bomb
spat out of that toothless zealous crater-mouth,
out of that virulent volcanic pumice-scatter of hell-fire talk
and abused feeling, I go on being the projectile.
I go on roaring up, trying not to notice,

(little man that I am, in my fantasy I weigh three
                    thousand pounds
and fleck off skins of blue fire as I boom in the middle
                    of the state fair)
I seem to be flying forever higher and higher,
—will I never come to rest?

And when I wake up late at night and think where am I,
and what is about to happen and who will help me,
and I don't know, I think
if only there weren't so much to love about them.
Where did it start, this anathema of the real?
One great-aunt who lived at the time of the war
wrote forty years ago "the life of the slaves with kind
masters and mistresses is an epic that causes the history
of the South to stand out in the history of nations
as unique as a lovely poem. And it has made me glad
twice; to have known it in its romantic beauty and to know
it had to end to wipe out that blot upon a nation's honor."
And my grandfather, remembering the same times,
seeing them with another eye of witness—
"Several times on my way to school I saw the body of a
criminal lying in the street, having received his just
deserts for his crime. I remember a bad and desperate
negro, Alex Mason, who was in jail—a company of
regulators went up to regulate him and he fought so
furiously they had to kill him. I remember the whites
and blacks rioting in the streets—"
Where did it start?
I suppose it was all in that forbidden fun,
for amusement and money,
when they sold the first cargo on the Congo.
Whisky for the chief, gold and women for the crew.

A fortune for the Portsmouth Puritan
commanding the brigantine.
All for fun—
And fun not being allowed for in the rules.

This is my South!
What do I do about it?
How do I get this belonging out of my belly?
Someone speaks of it,
there's a luckless minute when the anger goes away
and nothing is left but the Thanksgiving table,
the warm smells and the sounds of people,
the aunts, uncles, brothers, sisters,
fathers and mothers, all of them
eating and drinking, cracking the bones of life
in the name of Service and Our Father and Right.
All for fun, that isn't allowed for in the rules,
everything turning to moral service—like murder.
—To drink to forget we drink to forget we live.
My God, stop operating, Doctor Schweitzer,
putting that steel plate front to back in our heads.
It makes us able to go on drinking death
and never connecting with the taste of it.

George Washington's Mud

It's a great comfort to know this country had a father
and that he was as crazy as my father.
That with a presumption of faultless logic
he was able to get involved in a lifelong attachment to
                    that Potomac mud
trapped in the horseshoe bayous around his farm.

Damn it, he thought (I presume), his fields could feed
                    on that thick black
almost edible slime! And like the rest of us easy-to-humbug men
he thought anything he was able to reason out
was possible. A most endearing fallacy
                    like any number of mine.
Up in his workshop he contrived a machine
for making the river move—to float out the gravel
and leave the dirt. But he was as pragmatic as he was visionary.
While reason plotted, he worked a crew of slaves
in a sort of holy war on behalf of the land.

Of course he was always just about to be almost finished
                    (and happy)
till he caught the pleurisy that made him a finished monument.
The congressmen swarmed in out of the patronage lines
preparing posthumous lies to be brought out
about the honors, etc., appointments, the general had
                    or should have confirmed.

And they came trotting over when he seemed about to speak,
saying "any advice for the nation sir?" not wanting any,
                    really,
but willing to listen to the man.

Well, he sat up of course and made the fools get out of
                              his way like flies.
His last anger went off like a cannon.
It burst with a splash above the river bank.

"Look at that, gentlemen!—Look at that glorious mud!
That's what life is about, that mud!
And I shall get my hands on it, or perish!"
Which brought on a fatal convulsion and perfected his vow.
So he had a good death, happy, involved,
convinced he had just been washed by the logic of his century
to a glorious death in the battles of tides
                              and erosions and rivers.

Dying God

And what is the dialectic itself, but the naiveté
of an atheist trusting God's habitual way of doing things?
My God! Such a grabbing at greased pigs of words!
We're all atheists talking in the habit of God.

Because God was the first institution of our city,
systematically accreted with our statues,
lost in our law, just as he was written into our thousand treaties,
concreted into our towers of emotion, garbled with our music.

His temple has been mislaid again and again and reidentified
in the seventh level of the burnt cities below.
It was thought to be the shower-bath of a pederast merchant prince
whose big-buttocked ivory Goddess was on his ring.

But still he gyrates and ascends in our adventurous fall,
and it is his fervor we tranquilize with our ulcers.
The God of the west is our God. His jealousy
makes jealousy the kerosene of our jet.

He died at Nemi, Oeta, Calvary,
to stoke the fires of energy we burn.
Our hatred and remorse re-arrange his torture
to flog the furious engine into song.

There Used to Be Morning

There used to be morning.
Now there is six o'clock.

Dawn was like arrows.
Up, up rising
ringed with bubbles of shed light
crawling up the sky like a V,
and bursting into birds of passage.

There used to be morning.
Now there is six o'clock.

Even early the earth would begin to sink
faster and faster under me like a bed,
falling, under the curtains falling
and under the bedclothes falling,
trailing in air,
black clotting and gray,
heels over head into orange
down altogether
into an ocean of mile-deep purifying sun.

There used to be morning.
Now there is six o'clock.

Sun King

Without a single bone to pick or fratricidal thought,
I get off the bus at 5 p.m. and look out
at all the sky curled up like baroque,
curling and peeling into rococo,
filled with fat pearl-gold clouds like fire balloons,
floating across an enormous silk blue square of screen.

I take an incautious breath and slide off into that kind of upness
where there are ten million plump acres of afternoon,
planted and fanned by feathers of southwind—
I discover the secret of Louis Fifteenth's good time,
which floats like a pink fat cotton candy cloud
across the fleshy walls and ceilings at Versailles.

Then with a bump—and a spasm of light—it changes,
the same sky has become a red warm odalisque
cross-legged on her ottoman, plump cheeks gouged
with the pits of her fingers. There are red and yellow
diamonds in her tiles, and golden tassels
dangle from the cushions all about her of purple and black.

Then, with a crash!—shifts again, becomes a battle picture.
Shivers up in flames! Fire creeps out across piles of banners.
Red drapes and grenadier hats fall over.
Cartridge belts and parchment drums catch fire and flare.
Celestiality! I have discovered a new world!

I'll commence living in this landscape,
I'll find out what it's like to be a sun king at last,
to shine, to make fire processions about splendid palaces forever!
But before I can stretch out my one minute,
                    alread it's gotten too late.
As I watch, with a gulp, it all goes around and around
                    in a whirlpool,
and every bit of that wealth washes off down the drains
                    of the sun.

I Come In Late

I come in late. My daughter has gone to sleep.
There is an army of old shoes scattered,
they seemed like verve this morning,
tonight they have suddenly grown old.
There is a cold air from the window over her head,
she likes being friendly with the outside,
she is not so lonesome sleeping in my bed,
often she lies awake in the back
where her mother made her the princess bed with curtains
and stars, listening to the people next door
cursing each other. She says her mother told her
people's religion keeps them together
all life long, shouting at each other.
"I get lonesome back there with strangers" she says,
she misses her little brother complaining in the night.
She likes to see her mother twice a week
and has a witch who lives under her bed with a buzz-saw.
She has to twist and turn to protect her feet.
I wish I had a witch under my bed with a buzz-saw
who'd cut me clean in half while I was asleep.

POEMS AND TRANSLATIONS FROM

A Masque of Surgery

1974

A Journey

I was three years old
and I stepped up into the streetcar
while they thought I was taking a bath,
where I sat next to a lady who smelled like raspberries.
Instead, she smiled like a macaroon.
"I'm going to find my mother," I said.
"Jing! Jing!" said the bell.
The conductor knew where he would be going,
how could he fail, set like intention
on that shining parallel window-bar?
They asked me my name and I knew.
Trees and houses, gutters, motorcycles and cars.
So on ever since with never a stop.

A Masque of Surgery

I

Executed once more
in the treachery of the memory,
the drums filing scratches and forming ranks,
the bells coming up from beneath the cobbles,
flutes making way for the shimmering of bodies,
the fatal turns that rise backward to the command,
and fire.
And I sink once again into the fated
impossibilities of the past
and lie awaiting again that desperate *coup de grace,*
the feared memory that will not come.

II

Is it all a ballet, like a Napoleonic battle,
perfumed with the lubrications of blood
across the whistling fields of
popping and drumming provinces?
Are they reaching like us,
through implacable files of mechanical grenadiers
without legs, from general to general,
from hill to hill, from copse to copse,
from white horse to white horse
and drinking the final breath of brainless heroism
from cups of mouths like gasping wines
to make up the well-meant gift of animated death?

III

Or is it the cave that must be gone down into,
step under step
sliding across water through blackness,
sliding down wet bank after wet bank
into mile long rooms echoing with shrill water,
fifty miles under the kidneys of Bear Mountain?
And come back from, up crooked chimneys
lost among blind fish,
crawling elbow to elbow with newts,
shouldering aside foxes and shovels,
swiming through boulders
so that afterwards, no air, no sun
seems half so solid.

IV

Or is it how we'll sit in the crow's nest watching
fire ships spidering flame webs down the channel,
then the rigging flares
and the admiral who has gotten us into this,
through romantic sensibility and nervous honor,
has lost both legs,
and sits propped, roped, in a chair,
regulating the buckets in the proper order
how they are filled and thrown upon the correct flame.
It's a charade of hopelessness and nonsense.
We accept it for the sake of the shared values.
Or somewhat like Byron, wasting a life
of unnecessary despair because he will not
admit to himself
that what he really wants to love is boys,
but he has to live by the values of his time,

and no woman, no matter how beautiful or good,
can bind up the hemorrhaging wound of his soul.

V

What *is* the beginning?
Is it the tower, heavy as Babel,
swaying under Jupiter?
Where does the deep unlatch the height?
Is there a country big enough, in case it escapes?
Is there a place where someone operates,
climbing and rotating
the pedals of the bicycle-trepanning machine?
Where inner and outer converge like an eye,
in the ultimate tight knot of hip and thigh?
Where the wind comes unwinding,
and skin bellies like a sail.

VI

So at last, it's coming out! The pressure is there,
just above the right ear-lobe.
From there, faster, faster, the greens of parks
and country roads bore through the rocks of
the meaningless mountain
to the percussion room of fulminate waiting to explode!
And there! Lovely cataclysm!
Ah, the pressure is free!
And life roars out completely itself—
hear it whistling!
It runs downhill like burst-out water,
making for the imagination of the sea.

Whitman Saw It Crazily Shining

Whitman saw it crazily shining in his particular limbo,
All the while old dirty Europe died.
It gleamed over thick black tossing
oceans of impossibilities, saying
tie him to the rock,
split him under the knife,
some belief in Justice
can't be eviscerated out of man.

And here it comes again—over the ridge,
with band music, wisps of fife. The grass rattles.
—a forest of hats, bobbing in the grass line—
my many-colored mushroom army!
Someone is waving a blue rag.
Coming into sight are hundreds of shimmering
butterfly-colored banners
shot with flashes of flutes and piccolos,
darting up and down like bright fish,
climbing like Jacob's ladders into the light.

My raggle-taggle army,
coming along like gypsies, changing colors,
not marching to marches out of tune,
children on their shoulders chirruping
ta-ting, ta-boom,
walking against the music.
They wander a moment crosswise,
fragment and stream away to some other place.
Nothing in particular is there,
more than where they came from.
They're going there anyway, for the song.

Red Mountain

Tu Fu said
"I climbed west on Incense Burner Mountain
—I will erase the dust from my face
and live in the place I love
separated forever from the world of men—"
Sometimes I almost guess where that may be,
when the low, sheepflock clouds pass running
into the northeast and are caught
tumbling against the pinetops of the hills—
and above, the sunfish of the second layer high
are flattened and swim portly across to the South—
while the starlings, like smoke,
boil up out of the ruined Sycamores
and turbulent loblolly.
The Mammoth Silurian hummocks of the storm front
coast in brushing away the barely commencing stars.
It isn't here I thrive and belong
on this mechanized, macerated, staring sod,
but up in that turbulent
liquid element where everything is changing,
being blown from Mountain Rock to Endless Plain River,
to the past-changing of the sun and the moon.

Birmingham, 1973

What's That You Say, Cesar?

To Cesar Ortiz-Tinoco

The poet—a political animal?
Yes! Yes!
The way you said that phrase undressed me completely.
There I was naked in a painting of Orozco
holding up a torch which was my own
arm burning above the elbow.
And you yourself were Father Hidalgo
tolling the church-bell of Dolores,
pulling yourself straight up into the air
with your own emotion.
At a moment like that, who would not agree?
yes—yes—a poet is a political animal.

But he is as many other kinds of animal as possible, too.
A suffering animal—delegated
to take on the madness and feckless atrocity of us all,
and of everything.
A hungry animal.
Everything at which he looks with passion
he desires to eat.

A living animal—almost so much more alive
than he or anyone else can have the patience to endure.
A traveling animal, emitting and transmitting
Marquesas and Popocatapetls like bubbles in his afterglow.

A fighting animal. He is always down
at the back fence gathering handfuls of ass-manure.
He is able to throw three hundred yards

and strike his enemy in the eye without fail.
A capricious animal.
Here he is sniffing at the holes of bad fortune
and good fortune,
he is trying to decide which will taste better
and is worth digging out of the ground.
A lustful animal.
See how everything he looks at makes him either angry
or in love?

He is always down by the docks helping Venus
out of the sea to be raped.
He is always avenging her rape in a vertigo of righteous rage.

Backs and buttocks and breasts—
he is thrown into spells of deep breathing
and scalded imagination by backs and buttocks and breasts.
By the *idea* of backs and buttocks and breasts!
(male or female)
He falls away constantly
into snatches of mating dances and fertility incantations.

Well then, of course—
when he has been all these kinds of animal,
what you say, too.
Certainly he is in love with the idea of kings and queens,
also presidents, secretaries, first commissars,
leaders of communes, oligarchists and prime ministers.
He does not disdain dictators.
He has been one, he expects to be one again,
at the first overturn of the state.
Do you see that creature crawling below
about the ballot boxes, snuffling?
It is he.

Also that one standing on the balcony
eating up the cheers.
If there is anyone who loves justice he is there,
if there is anyone loves injustice,
he is there also.
He is in whatever place anyone lives or no-one.
Whatever gave you the idea he was any person in particular?
He was intended to be you.

Laughter

When Athena walled the furies up
in the Acropolitan cave,
it gave the signal
for Aeschylus to die
and Aristophanes to be born,
—Humor—the bastard son of Horror and Revenge—
and those Furies are locked up still—raging on,
in the Acropolitan cave of my side.

How they bang on my ribs,
scream "Everlasting Justice!"
scream "Now! Now! Now!"
in a walled up voice that sounds like Mickey Mouse,
while they grind, and pinch, and squeeze.

Didn't my Grandpa run away in a rage
and make himself a doctor
out of the tremor and gift of his ever-renewing fury?
Through his madness I see the funny side of things.

Three conscience-ridden generations
of duty, blood-bespattered mad adventure,
rolling with laughter,
never forgetting we'll go home in the end
to step-great-grandfather's house in Athens in Alabama,
and hold the cosmos up like a custard pie
and laugh and plop it in his face.

It's misery makes us funny.
The greatest unwritten farce is Oedipus,
the most hilarious people in the world
are Blacks and Jews.

Beethoven, broke, sick and deaf,
sets tubercular Schiller's Ode to Joy.
The Hebrew God
gets us down
and saws us open without anaesthetic,
to put that stitch in our side.
Finding a worm in the tree of Genesis,
he squashes it on his thumb
and calls it laughter.

Stonewall

That Last Day,
When he set himself at the reins
of a brand new horse, and reared,
(his wife said he looked like a hero of chivalry)
dressed as a gold braid comic general,
going along with Jeb Stuart's joke,
he knew it was funny.
He knew the men would laugh at him
for wearing it,
riding away to be shot.
The cliche makes more seamless legend,
that picture of Old Bluelight, all shoddy collar,
dirty cap, and snarling a prayer.

But he broke Virginia law
to teach his neighbors' slaves to read and write.
(One day a week every week)
because he thought the law was wrong.
The penalty was death.
And he almost—once—turned Catholic,
and stayed in Mexico and married a Spanish girl.
He toured the art museums of Europe for half a year.
Even in Lexington,
strapped in that horrible, nervous
jail of a military mission,
drawing the shades to spare the Presbyterians,
he danced the whole night through,
without any music except his own,
to Miss Amelia.

The Don Quixote of the Kitchen Table

The day I set out,
Knight of the Most Unimportant Armor,
Sancho would not follow.
Had he guessed so early what was meant?
My Rosinante found her way home—even hobbled.
The minute I let my eyes close
I was run over by sheep.
Looking the other way,
thinking about a star, I have been attacked by windmills.

Still—forward, friends!
Perhaps in a country of miracles and giants,
we may discover our honor.
Can you remember anything about its size?
I mention it faithfully in my battle cry.
I vaunt I'll war on Troll or Turk at any stake
to maintain it is fierce and true
and inconsolably ours (though who knows where?)

So, friends, I've told you what I am and do.
Onward! Onward!
The devil with pros and cons!
Who sinks his spurs in facts
is already lost.

Grandpa

If I got rich, what would I say about it to Grandpa?

Here we are taking a ride
in the buggy.
I am five years old.
He is eighty-eight.
Over the bluff to the farm to show me the cherry trees.
Old Starlight chop-chops,
hind-quarters stretching like chewing,
in my face. I'm amazed to see the great black
hundred violin bows of horsehair fling up
frantically as the whole insides
(the insides of a horse!)
pucker up and out and plop away
hay brown balls of sparrow dinner,
all up and down the bird-happy road.

Or I put my finger on a place at Chickamauga
where in 1863
he is firing his rifle out of the chink of his eye
from the cow-top powder horn
that hung in my closet while I was growing up;
getting away a shot or two
before somebody is hurt,
then turning away
to open the black square surgeon's kit
worn white on the corners,
and chop and lay open and probe—
making faces—
Why—begin the incision—
did his mother marry the hateful son of a bitch?

—saw the bone—why did he have to trot
beside the buggy like a dog?
—drop the arm in the bucket—why did he run away
and make a doctor on his own?—why have to?

He loaned out all he had on notes of hand.
A gentleman repays,
and if a gentleman does not,
then write on the ledger he tried.
And though he had a lot of property once,
—biggest taxpayer, Giles County, Tennessee, 1912,
he died tough, and calm, and greatly owed,
with he didn't give a damn what faithless paper.

Snail

translated from the Spanish of Federico Garcia Lorca

They have brought me a snail.

Inside it sings
of a sea of maps.
My heart
fills with water,
with little fish,
silver and brown.

They have brought me a snail.

The Mute Boy

translated from the Spanish of Federico Garcia Lorca

A little boy's looking for his voice.
(It's a captive of the King of the Crickets.)
Inside a droplet of water
a little boy is looking for his voice.

I'm not looking for it to speak with,
I want to make a ring of it
to wear like a setting, my silence,
on my littlest finger.
Inside a droplet of water
a little boy is looking for his voice.

(The captured voice, in a far away place,
is putting on the clothes of a cricket.)

A Goodbye

translated from the Spanish of Federico Garcia Lorca

If I die,
leave my balcony open.

A little boy's eating oranges.
(With the balcony open I see him.)

The harvester harvests the wheat.
(With the balcony open, I feel it.)

If I die,
leave my balcony open.

I Want to Turn to the South: 1941

translated from the Spanish of Pablo Neruda

From a sick bed in Veracruz I remember a day
of the South in my own country, a silver-plated day
like the quickest fish in the waters of heaven.
Loncoche, Lonquimay, Carahue, whose heights
are scattered about ringed with silence and roots,
like watchmen from their thrones of leather and timber.
The South is a great horse sunk like a stone
crowned with slow-moving trees and dew,
as though lifting his green snout hanging with waterdrops.
The shade of his streaming tail is a great archipelago
and in his intestine sprouts the miraculous coal.
Will you never more talk to me, darkness, never more, oh hand,
never more talk to me, oh foot, threshold, thigh, my struggle—
and startle the forest, the highway, the ear of wheat,
the mist, the cold, that like azure, decided
which of your ceaseless steps should accomplish itself?
Sky, summon up a day when I move through star on star
trampling the light like fireworks, wasting my blood
till I come to the nest of the rains.
                              I ask to go
back of the timber of the river, the musky
Tolten, let me pass by the sawmills,
and enter the cantinas my feet soaked with water,
guide me past the light of the hazelnut's electricity.
Lay me out full length in the excrement of cattle
to die and revive gnawing at the wheat.
                              Ocean, bring me
a day of the South, a day gripped in your waves,
a day of wet trees, brought by a wind
of azure, out of the pole, to my ice-bound banner.

Your Eyes

translated from the Spanish of Octavio Paz

Your eyes are the country of lightning and tears
the silence that belongs
to the storms without wind, a sea without rollers,
caged birds, gilded animals sleeping
topaz as sacrilegious as truth,
autumn in the clearing of the forest whose light
      sings in the shoulder of a tree,
and all the leaves are birds.
Shore that the meeting of the morning
will cover with eyes like stars,
basket of fruits of the fire,
the lie that nourishes,
mirror of the world, doorways of the beyond,
tranquil beating of the seas at high noon,
wink of the absolute,
Alpine plain.

Violence of the Hours

translated from the Spanish of Cesar Vallejo

They've all died.
Dona Anna's dead, the boastful lady who made cheap
bread in the town.
Santiago the Curate is dead, who was pleased
when the young men and the girls greeted him,
answering everybody indiscriminately
"Good morning, Jose! Good morning, Maria!"
Carlota is dead, pretty red-haired thing, leaving behind
a baby of three months old who almost at once, died also,
only eight days after her mother.
My Aunt Albino is dead, who sung of old times and customs
in the country, sewing in the corridors
for Isabel, who was only her maid, but the most
                    honorable of women.
Old One-eye is dead, I can't remember his name, but he slept
in the sun in the morning, sitting in front by the door
of the tinsmith at the corner.
Rayo is dead, the dog as big as I am,
of a gunshot wound, nobody knows by whom.
Lucas is dead, my brother-in-law in the peace of belts,
whom I think of when it's wet and there's nobody
part of my experience.
My mother is dead in my revolver,
my sister in my fist, my brother in my bloody guts,
the three linked by the saddest kind of sadness,
in the month of August of year after year.
Mendez the musician is dead, tall and terribly
drunk, doing runs of sad toccattas upon his clarinet,
at whose articulations the hens of my
neighborhood used to go to sleep, long before the time
for the sun to go down.
My eternity is dead, and I keep vigil over it.

POEMS FROM

The Trash Dragon of Shensi

1978

Flute and Specs

George Washington played the flute.
Benjamin Franklin wore octagonal specs.
Betsy Ross hem-stitched a jingo flag
with a brummagem needle.
Where Madoc landed at Mobile Bay
to found Welsh Kingdoms
came an admiral dreaming a dirty word
for a dance of confederate barrels.
Thoreau slept a year by a lake
in the hot-dog stand
where Shakespeare married his wife
for her aura of thatching.
It came about that his thumb-stitching father
was fined for exuberant trash.
They stopped Aaron Burr
from plotting an empire, in Alabama,
and built an asylum on the spot
for black-skinned madmen
wild with dreams of being free.
Gypsy trippers eat their eggs
where Druids met and Caesar cut their trees.

It's all historical freak and confused.
It's all bunk, as Henry Ford said,
licking his finger and fixing a truck.
All horse-play and optical tricks
and Prescott and Gibbon and Plutarch run in the rink
and scatter and duck like the rest
as the bullets fly
at the meeting of Billy the Kid and Tom Mix.

Bill Where Are You?

I think of you racketing
around Birmingham astride our purple Henry J,
busted door lashed shut,
and running a bowling alley out
Mountain Brook way.
Still, I'm convinced once more we're going
to put up a house on the Southside.
But Schatzi says we're not.
That it happened again.

The first time, they thought you were drunk.
You spent ten hours
in the city tank, bless your infarcted heart,
and sued the council.

The only carpenter-plumber
I ever heard of who loved ballet,
started life as a dealer of 21
in the Loop of Chicago,
acted in plays, studied at school
with the Syndicate's odds maker,
and every year got four week's work
as Santa Claus.

I remember we made a practise barre
for Richard and Gage,
and one day Schatzi wrote and said
you wouldn't come home any more.

Once you said, to hit the jackpot,
catch a woman square upon the cervix.

You caught her.
But she hadn't caught you anywhere.
You were still most happy thinking
of bumming drunk and free
about the two-foot snow
of the blizzard of '48 in Illinois.

18 months you came every day,
you helped remake my house.
I don't know why, there wasn't any money.
Maybe you needed like faith
to be useful at anything.
You kept me from going insane.
That's all I wanted to say.
Except—sleep well.
I can't figure out for the life of me
where you've gone.

(for William Gaither 1917–1966)

Becoming

Anthropologist marries tribal chief—headline

Half of whatever we are lives a life
somewhere else nobody told us about.
How did we become committed to something
no one explained? What we understand
about the very beds we sleep in
or the houses we stay shut up inside
is the texture of the wood and the cloth.

Was this woman, student of the tribes, marrying her tribal chief—
the lone, ugly fat girl
unable to be the Miss America of one culture,
claim-jumping to another? No,
it's only order beginning again
its dumb tireless effort to overtake the universe.

It's the disciple becoming the discipline.
Anthropology coming to life in the anthropologist.
Just as the president strains
to become a political monument,
and the priest hopelessly entangles himself with God.
The zoo keepers keep finding less and less
to tell themselves from the lemurs.

In the same way, the actors keep vanishing into the play,
and on a cliff an ornithologist flaps,
already halfway a bird.
We are marrying what we study by.
It's a fountain of anarchy crowned with a summit of oneness.
Oh lucky physicist, Dantean traveler,
high in the ionosphere,
busy becoming the light!

Dr. Freud

It's a small room with a white institutional chair,
three lights overhead, an enamel table full of instruments.
Dr. Freud sits on the flowering pad of the seat,
his daughter Anna has just begun to insert
the artificial rubber throat
by which alone he can swallow and talk.
It is inhumanly hard,
her face is taut with merciless force.
He has told her don't insult me with sympathy,
otherwise stay out of the fitting room.
That is why her face remains immobile except for the strain
and the sweat beads on her forehead.

His firm feet in high shoes sit there rigidly,
his eyes are closed, his forehead mottled and red,
his beard anonymous.
Nothing else in sight lets show the underpinning of anarchy.
The linoleum floor is spotless,
the mail on the hall table
visible outside, is piled on a tray.
Through the door at the other side of the hall is a desk
covered with Cypriot horses, Gods from Ur,
eighth-century Greek herms,
Hellenistic Apollos, lyre waiting to be strung.

Choir

Watching myself wag along
Wondering how I got this far—
with the head making book on a horse
not in the foot,
and the farmer in the left hip
arguing with the town in the bone.

The boot emperor sneers at the hand workman,
the stomach's wandering monk is bored
with the sensual nose.
The girl in the eye
sneers at the boy in the groin
who is busy strangling the old man in the tongue.
Ah clever conductor!
I thought I heard a single voice
when I was young.

Waiting for the Leonids

The first time they came, in 1833,
my! What a devil of a fright!
Cows ran away in the fields,
farmers fell down on their knees
cursing a rich man's impractical God
that went and arranged for Judgment Day
right after the harvest—making all the work go for nothing.

There was a burlesque actress in New Haven
took remorse and became a traveling revivalist.
She toured the Midwest out of Chicago
advertised with a musical pig.
Mothers looked on their babies for starry birthmarks.
In North Dakota a cow gave birth to a spotted goat,
Athabascans did the sky dance.

No fear of any of that now—
we know they're only six bits
of loose comet dust sweeping around the sun
like a galactic rain or mist.
When the drops of peripheral fire
begin to spout from the East,
we stand up, not at all surprised.

Suddenly the sky
like a hydrant, foams with streams of stars.

Shock! Whiz! they soundlessly dagger
all about us like grindstone sparks,
breaking through
the safety encrusted mother of our sky—
We begin to look uneasily at one another.
Who the devil are you, anyway?
Whose tears are running down whose faces?

Thank You for the Language

For the use of the words,
the speech that drives me,
to those who have died
going before in the duty of attention,
with whose feet I walk
and on whose shoulders I am carried.
What do they care?

It's for my own sake I say I will be
a house that is not burned down.
And forever rest in the house
of those who do the same,
and will take up loads
larger than can be borne
for the bravado of it.

It pleases only me to remember
how the monks of Seville
beginning a cathedral by the Giralda
vowed upon their chapter minutes
to build so great a thing
to the glory of God
that those coming after
would think they were mad to attempt it.

Boy

He hops down the moldy step
of the nearby rotting tenement
about ten, like a rude sparrow,
crutch grabbed in the right shoulder pit.
The nub of the leg underneath
is stitched up over the flap of the knee.
In the left hand he turns a baseball bat,
throws it in the air,
catches it at the twirl.

I've seen him somewhere before,
I think it was night, by Alice Tully Hall,
racing in the lights of the swiveling cars.
He flew his canted-over-to-the-side bike
past us all down Columbus into Ninth,
one foot driving the wheels
with a scattering of sparks.
Zing! Zing! whizzing like a bolt.
And the crutch, braced on his shoulder,
flipped over against the skyline's nose
like a thumb.

Frog

I've known the flesh was correct
from the first day of being delivered into it.
Whatever the finger, the fleabite,
the aching wound, the round prepuce,
the pink pee-cave
of the black girl in the alley
signaled,
it was in the sense of the running dog,
the flapping fish, the unerring Flicker,
and registered on an organ of exactness
in the eye of right.
If I were reversed into some kind
of ritual sinlessness
in the worm-pit of the abstract,
I'd come hurtling out like a flying frog,
and leaping, sprawling,
claim my birthright and show who I was
and croak my animal outrage
over the pond of fact.

Me

I keep trying to tell you about myself,
but it is so clever,
even as I spread the noose
snick! it flies through the barn door.
And there is a pair of oars against the blue
swimming as high as I can see.

I turn in a hurry, trying to catch
that party who was pinning on my tail.
Sailor, I say, movie-actress-actor,
King Tut of the camera,
always black in the film,
who are you hoodwinking this week?
I was hoodwinking nobody.—I looked.
There was nobody to hoodwink.

The Trash Dragon of Shensi

There was an ancient worm
on the hills of Shensi
which had six spines upon its back
that flowed red when it flew
at the Spring moon,
ballooning and unballooning its awful wings
in the brick-hearted sun.

Now it has been caught.
They climbed the rootless cliffs
beyond Sian
(they were very brave and very determined)
and someone flung the silken ropes
while he was sleeping,
(dreaming of water and cloud spouts)
over the spiny angles of his rough heads
steaming like fire hydrants.

They damped him with fog,
and a promise of the disklike moon
for his own on Mondays.
They led him with milk.
And now he toils.
He is the eater of garbage for a whole prefecture.
He is known to every corner
as the Trash Dragon of Shensi.
And he is too full of old watermelon rinds
and millet straw to pay any attention
to his wings.

Only in sleep,
vibrating his spiny reptilian pinions,
does a little steam nicker about his nozzle,
does he buzz a little, throb a little like a train.
He is thinking of red searchlights
in a fishlike moony sky,
and the mountains looking like
great flopped-over turtles below
weaving their legs and heads.

But he no longer believes in flight.
He has accepted his silken attachments.
He has even come—almost—
to believe in the ultimate dignity
of the transmutation
of fish bones and broken squash pods.

The People of My Head

The people of my head
are whiners and spongers every one,
roughnecks and armed private detectives.
Who were born to be saints.
Every after-midnight they hold conventions,
caterwauling insults and obscenities,
boiling up washpots of tar and feathers.
When I've arranged for them
to walk quiet timber between woodpeckers
shimmering among moony clearings,
they stay indoors
posting shootouts on bar-room bulletin boards.

Why have I been chosen for their raucous conclaves?
When I left them for good, once,
they forced themselves on the train
and sat between me and the windows
shouting, pawing each other's dirty sandwiches,
fouling each other's pocket recorders with "shits."

I have wanted to be the kind of man
who entertains good company.
Who found these vulgar people to invite?
I am a country overrun with cheap American tourists,
they are befouling my mountains,
my water is brown, and in the museums and schools
the pictures are punched and black with thumb-prints.

Once I declared myself a monastery,
nothing was allowed to ring but matins.
Not three hours passed
before the local whores were taking their customers
into the sacramental arches under the lamps,
and the monks baking the paschal bread
bartered their flour for firewater,
lay down with their cassocks up to their navels
and loaded the ovens with chalk.

One Man, One Vote

I used to follow with astonishment
the goings and comings of famous statesmen and politicians,
George Norris, La Follette,
Citizen Lincoln, Tom Jefferson (fabulously managing to die
in Virginia the same day John Adams died in Boston
—on the Fourth of July).
Oh our revolution, not since you flagged out
has any admiration been so brightly bannered!

Here came Roosevelt, the man of the blue eagle,
throwing bolts at evil, lightning in his claws!
Or Daniel Webster, gargling thunder!
Surely, God meant something like this
when he invented heroic love.

Then, I discovered
none of all of it had anything to do with goodness.
They—all of them—were monsters
of zeal, of idealism, like me,
even egotistical, got up of self-interest.

Great clay, damn, booby feet,
size sixteen—if they were no better
as liars and pretenders
than I was, who was there left, anywhere,
to look up to greatly, like a holy mountain,
and reverently, from afar, see?

The big bird flew squawking over the mountain
with shivering black wings.
When will it come back, pinfeathers glistening
red white and blue?
Until it does, I simply make my mark.
I keep my heart locked up
in a ballot box with a brass key.

I Want to Have Been the Shaman

I want the people to come to me
and say "Oh brother,
make us a new woodpecker dance!"
And sleep on it and have the thing come down to me
in a dream and shake my knees
like a shaggy knees of a spirit.

Savage?—the Ojibwa or the Mandan?
Friend, they are far less savage than you.
For do they not know who they are?
You have not even begun to find out.

I want the sum of us to be at most a hundred,
I want us to be at one with the earth
and everything we can see of the Universe.
The rest we can populate out of our own
most wildly exciting improbabilities,
living by our hands and our own will
among the beans or on the buffalo plains.
My dances will last hours and win wars.
Give me something my size!

Look at this!—Poor lost fistful of medicine!
Wasting from between my fingers like sand.
Though I am crammed like a bursting ear with songs,
I run off the swale of wasted power.
Rhythm is all the healing I have, brothers
—rhythm—
waiting here in the dark corner with drum and rattle.
And no one to heal.

Here! Here!

Anything I am not a part of
I do not want to happen.
When you tip your hat
to the vast crowd
be sure you look at me.
I am here,
do not walk by
and pretend you thought
there was nothing.
Whoever you wanted
and were looking for,
here I am!
here I am!
I am he!

Santa Claus is coming down from the winter,
a wind is knocking up in the flue,
boots are making chips in the chimney,
I hear the grinding of his back.
I am waiting below,
he is about to shinny the last foot down,
where he will sneeze, grunt,
blow his nose,
get down on his hunkers,
and undo the string at the neck of his sack.
I am about to go mad.
I jump and hold my breath.
I am in his pack.

My Father Invented the Submarine

It's the last report we shall have.
In a moment or two, you will rise,
you will lift the fiberglass hatch
above the steel cone,
stretch vertically the long iron grille
built with your hand-made impregnable
bars of honor and grit
—hesitate—
make ironical bows to the harbor, to the clouds,
—to us—and climb in
and down, and lower the hatch
above you like a lock.

Shutting out
the daily obscenity,
the wastage of mean thought,
the slither underfoot of superficial manners,
the daily lies of refreshment and love,
the sneaking, ambitious, flatworm-hearted sky,
and be off—to adventure, surely,
nervously twisting the dials
about you—sinking in the emerald foreshore,
like a rock.

Where have you gone, daddy,
down there?
Are you cruising, sliding, somewhere beneath the sunless sea,
and riding along hallooing corridors,
glowing like a phosphorescent bead,
inside of me?

I think I see you, even hear you,
slowly floating deeper, deeper, grating upon
the center of myself, on my soul's sea floor,
aground upon the black reefs of your wrecked science.
Are you at one, finally,
or falling into one of the old mad unaccepting rages
to find yourself helplessly aground again
in the most unacceptable place of all places, trapped—caged like a
beast—
at least for a while—
bound in the hateful burning place of flesh,
locked, blocked, chained, and barred
for as long as I am to be myself,
in the unsurrendering humanness of my heart.

A Choice

About Sophocles, brought into court,
lately ninety years of age, witness after witness
tells them his wit is wandering.
The oldest son, seventy, thinks
he will have the inheritance at last.

But the old man, for his defense,
chooses to read a new play
about Colonus and whether
a resolution is possible between Gods and men.
He stands, his voice grows strong,
he becomes lost in the struggles of piety and will.
The magistrate suspends the hearing to weep.

After a lifetime of proving,
his is the pride that does not flicker a minute,
proving itself again.

But Socrates, when they give him the horror to drink,
tops it off with a smile and a wink
(though always as proud a man as they had)
and gives them what they think is the game
in the name of the game.

POEMS FROM

I Am the Jefferson County Courthouse

1981

I Am the Jefferson County Courthouse

It's safe in my head—clacking that typewriter, striking and
               singing,
across my temple—belonging nowhere else on earth
               anymore
but my press room, my courthouse, being enlarged in my
               amazement.
Yes—Sheriff MacDowell sits there
looking out the wide window of his basement,
resting both rough-shod feet on a 50-year-old roll-top
imaginary desk, hiccupping amidst the cigar smoke.
He is thinking—all over this county
deputies are serving warrants, five dollars a service,
in mud-spattered old Fords,
investigating murders, socking the suspects,
thinking up dumb answers to give
to smart defense attorneys showing off for juries,
buying Camels from bootleggers
in falling-down general stores covered with Retonga signs,
their sinks of galvanized iron set
on tanks of seething smelly mash.
He's thinking of this network of crime
sluicing for miles to Warrior and Birmingport—
as he watches—his eyes closed, he knows all,
like the Sphinx, he does nothing, thinks everything.
Like the Sphinx, his nose is eaten away by acne.

Every morning the black ladies in blue domestic,
the white-trash ladies in phony leopard-skin
are hurrying past in my head, twittering like barnswifts
in the flyway, blocking the passage to Judge Boner's court,
getting ready to call each other "bitchy,"

to stand in a circle shouting "yessir" to the prosecutor,
puffing out his throat there, glaring power,
his skinny rump on the desk of the shorthand clerk.
This is his lily pad, from which he addresses
a green pond of obedient bullfrogs. They crouch out front,
waiting for him to signal. Then they will sing.

Today, the judge tells him—you—be quiet now—
the judge is going to speak—
it's Decoration day, he will deliver the annual oration.
All year long he crouches behind that bench.
Now we shall see what he looks like!
Resting his pear-shaped paunch like a ripe fruit
on his blotter, he does not mumble
"case dismissed for lack of evidence"
or "$25 and costs, pay the clerk."
Today, instead, he remembers how he was a doughboy,
and what a privilege, to be this crowd of citizens we are,
star-spangled over by that mighty, motionless
banner gathering coal-smoke there!
We gawk. He spits, then sits down.
The Chairman of the Democratic Committee
is now to be bound over for rigging election returns—
and the drivers of two tow trucks are standing there to
                              be fined
for shooting it out at a traffic accident with signal flares,
and standing together to punch the highway patrol.

Here comes the governor's nephew, charged with sodomy!
Hooray!—case dismissed for lack of evidence!
Still, there is much more ready to be brought up
in the cockpit of my divided remembrance—how, far up—
past the tallest elevator, each with its paraplegic
                              doughboy,

veteran pilot soaring like a hawk, we fly to the solicitor's
                              aerie!
His office with its weary view of stars and coke convertors,
of Woodrow Wilson Park below and beyond, the lair
of his gloating nemeses across the way in City Hall.
There's nothing between us and Heaven but the jail,
with the prisoners overhead to keep us humble.
(He requests them not to sing.)
We never hear them, we always know they're there.
This is our Mr. Perry, he spares a moment for us always
in our dreams, out of his jinxed war with evil and Bull
                              Connor,
senility and Judge Wheeler, all those multiple
assaults of intractable human nature,
the surprises of the hundred kinds of dumbness
ready to fall on you from behind with a leaded weight.
And I think—it's the burden of being too bright
gives him wrinkles and tired soft patches about the eyes
—that he cares about things—that he softly, kindly
asks us what can be done for us today. Being honest
he knows there is nothing much
either of us could ever do for the other.
Both of us wonder why.

In a quiet corner of the imagination there is a press room,
filled with black machines.
Out the window is a giant lintel, over the east door.
A workman is innocently embracing a farmer, and both
rest and malinger under the knee of the brawny lady
blindfold, and by that token, called by everyone Justice.
Press Room!—my heart folds under—den of ancient
falling apart clickety-clackety typewriters.
Place of never resting more than a minute.
Always we hurry again down yellow, terrazo, Talladega

Marble floors
clacking our heels, to the Deputy's washroom
—off to read the latest graffiti—
which tells me somebody—is sleeping with his own
daughter,
that's today's news—and has since she was thirteen,
and she's a wonderful screw,
would anyone else come along to join and let him see?
And after that we stop for coffee to talk with a Chancery
Judge.
He just today disposed of twenty-five million dollars.
—We come away all silvery feeling, toe to chin.
—And sit and think about it all, over lunch.
There in my head these persons and places
take on their own life, assort themselves
in their appointed directions and positions—
to the east, the jittery plasterfaced highway patrolman
checking new drivers, hoping they'll not
collapse him beneath a turning postal van.
To the north, Jimmy, the Deputy Coroner,
driving to work with photos of gunshot heads and slashed
throats.

—Through the revolving door of the courthouse
junior clerks escaping for coffee with plump legal typists,
and even this moment, perhaps, the Chairman
of the Personnel Board—meditating whether to call the
County Auditor
—dolt—bindleheaded ass!—for a front page fight!
Off to the west, the red and white calla lilies
nod shyly under the tulip and locust trees
whispering like so many bored distracted gentry.
The litigants burp, wad the paper from lunch.
To the south, Miss Frances Mallom's students

SOMEONE WILL GO ON OWING

sing see-saws and ladders up in the Ridgeley.

Unchanged, in that Press Room I have by me,
Ed Strickland is busy typing out a scoop.
He's scooping us, what do we care?
Tomorrow we'll scoop him.
The creaky machine is flying,
cranking out the lies and appearances,
the happenings that have nothing to do
with what is really going on that you can see—
I sit there and make the novel of my memory.
We are all the plots.
Innocent of compassion or desire or greed
—see, we've finished, we type two stars
at the bottom of the page. Life! Life!
Captured at last, tied with an inky ribbon.
We exult and crack our heels.
Something is knocking upon our head upon the door.
Laughing, the copy boy comes in and cracks his gum.

—See, we've finished, we type at the foot two stars.

* *

Hilarity and Happiness

We're all laughing, riotous as sunlight and color,
under the oaks in the back yard with the comic dog.
But even doing our best, reality enters, mining under the
                    grass
like a digger with a lamp or an actor with a torch,
saying this lady with the lovely Spanish bones
is near to death. We do our best to pretend not to hear.

And also pretend not to know
that her husband, happy-go-lucky today as an unfenced bull,
will soon be doddering beef,
reduced to a scarecrow hung from his own spine.
We'd like not to have to think at all of such earnest lovers,
endlessly touching fingers and toes,
scattering tears in each other's hair,
or the alimony life they rashly live
like a burnt pair of moths,
frightenedly brushing the lamps of jail.

But can we be blamed?
What worthy thing's to be made of this much distress?
We've radiated joy as much as we could,
our laughter wildly fills up the patio,
rattles the happiness berries up in the trees,
absurdly enrages the unhappy slum-yard children next door
who hoot a kind of raucous despair, their hatred erupting,
to mark such a lustrous scene.

We wish we could help them tell
—or even explain to ourselves
what mark makes happiness happy.
How it differs in sign
from transmuted rage—and shining despair.

Sing Song

Yes, lark-footed in the chewing gum,
singing to come unstuck,
chanting like a mouse in king's boots,
on cat the master's carpet of cheese,
knowing in the end it's bound to come to grief.

Buzzing, making cells like bees
that are bound to be coarsely wrecked by sumptuous bears.
Stuffing berries with seeds
for somebody else to pick.
Rolling iron rations out of oats
for a horse that bites.

Giving your arm to be the flute
to a band of whistling mosquitos,
but saying, even while played upon,
what luck to be singing!
If only as someone's dumb lunch
in the kingdom of marrow.

Amelio's Power

That power you're only given
for not asking it,
I hope to find someday, leaning against my door.
But while I wait, I stand
at the entrance to Ali Baba's cave
twisting a fork of hazel till it splits,
and hear how the bowels of nothing snicker at me.

I know as well as anyone
water can never cry here! here!
But I want it—using its magic—to tell me so.

Amelio, whose daily job is barber,
takes a twig
in thick fists as though grown out of the weft
of the earth that in his weaving sings—
like a loop of power coiled in a place of somnolent
        corn—
like the noise of a conchshell full of the roar of the sea—
or like a map that shines in the ground—of a vast geode,
and without any guile,
he carelessly lifts some latch of the world
I can't see.

I long for his power—
for Nothing to find in my domain
a well down which to lean and summon up
those things which I abandon as I go.

Little Hero

Little hero, that's lifting up rivers
across one shoulder,
moving off mountains of horse-muck,
washing out dead air
from closed yellow caves.
Oh prestidigitator,
that's whisking scarves
from grey and brown to yellow and green and red,
making in a wink
two elephants and two giraffes
out of one,
painting giant swashes of blue
from gable to gable.
Sneaking in the houses,
coiling underneath the beds of lovers,
thriving upon their gigglings and lockings.
Locksmith of laughter,
unspringing the bolts,
kicking off the doors,
swallowing the keys,
ripping blankets
from the hill shoulders,
stretching out the green sheets,
smoothing them flat,
pouring out oceans of soda water
tumbling with seals.
Immortal hero, indestructible magician,
gossip and love-maker
—Spring!

Gulliver

To be little,
five foot seven—
yet love the Giant's daughter—
brilliant, beautiful,
moving up there like the Tower of Flaming Oil,
she puts the vast fingers of apocalypse
to her terrible lips with the bottomless taste
of the daughter of God.
She is just what heaven always wanted for you—
forty feet of grace
laughing up there out of reach.
Maddened, you leap sideways on the piano,
bang the mallets in rage and clamor,
you play love songs like cannon blows.
(You skid at the end of the diapason in your own tears,
or her sympathetic ones.)
She does her goodhearted best,
almost drowns you against her cheek.
You try to claw your way inside and sleep there for good.
What is there to do about it?
At best your arms will reach about her ear.
Oh hellish, old, wild, ever-repeated joke.
I've known it.
I've wept along with you, surgeon and brother.
I've understood it from the very beginning
without having to have it explained.

Tick Tock

Was it with Grandpa or Robert Frost
I rode out to look for the way we lost?
I remember one had a beard, and one did not—
but which one?
One spoke with a stutter of gold,
and one had an aim—
which one?
—And one had a guilt.
And where has that single-tree gone
I remember they said they built?
And what of the pride and the grudge and the blame
—what of them?
All mixed up in a pile I can dimly see
through the keyhole there on the shelf.
What are these objects? The shapes are strange
and rough.
I try to imagine how they saw them once.
Even as I look and try to guess their names
—twang!
Their pinhole into the past
is already closing itself.

Doubleknit Socks

Though I wear doubleknit socks and haberdashers'
                                marvels,
read portentous abstracts of disease,
stand like a plastic scarecrow square in the fields of study,
listen through the whistling cracks of tubes,
nothing I do important is my neighbor,
underneath I walk spells without shoes.

What runs through my sense cannot be canned.
There is an animal scuffling up my chimney
lighting fires of logs I do not control.
There is a creature shuffling in my basement
sleeping his sleeps and wakes by clocks
of rocks and seas I cannot find the setting to.

I Came into Life Cain

I came into life Cain
not because I asked it
but because I was born in Genesis.

In my turn I hated, was filthy
and reveled in dirt
thinking of murder
because they said God made us so.
That was all very well.

But when I turned like the beast
they said I was not
and tried wildly to lick
from the blue sky
its prickly painful stars
with my tongue,
I did that on my own.
Because I knew better—
that this was furious meat
and curious
and it wanted to know.

Plato

When I was born, Plato,
wanting to snare me for his own
with a few cheap gewgaws,
secretly placed a shiny conundrum in my left hand,
but as he did so,
unwarily sneezed, and my father caught him.

He looked, my father said,
like an alchemical doctor in a long black robe
(with crossed blue eyes).
Daddy, proudly waving an army issue forty-five,
thought he'd driven the madman away
with no harm done.

But everywhere I go,
I walk and look a little askew,
shine with an unearthly double, equivocal glow.
And I've three seals of a one-sided partnership—
the gap between my two front teeth,
a craving for salt—and a weak left thumb.

Lately, the victory flags
turn to tattered rags on calcareous stubs,
and I know he's returned.
He's hidden the apple of immortality
in my left fist.

That explains the shine.
But oh, of devious double mind,
he has smeared it with butter, so he may whisper *hubris*
as I bungle it away at the last pinch,
with the double-jointed thumb.

Machine of Years

You're at the Empire Building
thinking nothing's to worry about
but getting your picture taken, so I must run away
in the streetcar and make you meet me,
with lots of police and reporters
so I can yell like a three-year-old
"Where were you, why didn't you come?"

You see, nothing changes.
Another time your name is Jane,
you have freckles
just arrived from hearing Pinza
sing Figaro.
You tangle your long skirt in the clutch
trying to drive while I push,
and we're narrowly missed by a bus.
I howl three nights in a row
when you tell me about the guy from Colorado.

—You see?—Always reaching out to grasp
disappearing backs, which when I reach for them
are only your face.
You prepare me for the naive Russian poets
who talk of Man's purity,
saying it out of the squalor of prisons and Arctic camps.

You teach me how the important things we do
ring like pennies thrown to a beggar.
Funny, how through you, I have
always understood getting out of dungeons.

But something is wrong.
There I am, already fifty, reversed at the controls,
and you are only at the age when you got married.
Jupiter goes, revolving pole over pole,
and the sun's a baton twirler. I go up and up
shining as I am slung.
Yes, a mistake,
but isn't it always a mistake? Doesn't each of us speak in an unknown
language
using the same words?
I only wanted to bring you a little music
and my fingers were too gnarled.
Violent desire makes experience hang onto life!

Never mind, I did listen, and
fiercely noting what you tried to teach me,
I always left cracked in the roof
a secret door
to snatch with my fist at a star and miss.

Ducks

You've been hearing him from everywhere
for five minutes, and now
splitting the mist overhead, he wavers
like a sinuous single arrowhead
uncertain where to aim.
Barely missing the mountain, he flaps free.
But from behind him,
still concealed by cloud
comes a chaotic noise—
and intermittently bumbling into sight, they come,
a wild circus of drunken fowl
climbing all over each other
up, down, and around the sky.

Your hair roots clutch
even though you can hardly distinguish what
to feel!
Animals are not people
to them you apologize,
but you can almost hear the lost leader insisting
"I know where I'm going"
and with discordant whoop and
squawk
they jostle and flap at his rump
"We're coming! Wait!
Oh how we believe in you!"

A City

1982

A City

Running from the pestilence,
bringing it with me,
ringing in a waist-high Henry J like a peal of bells,
I went flapping with my daughter, dog, and friend,
whistling North from the South
locked in a feckless peanut streamer,
dragging a fierce and impossible freight
that was bounding before and behind
like an automatic piano waltz.
So we staggered around and far away
through Amboys and Bayonnes of flaming forts
(but the bridge like a ring with a diamond,
rusted off right,
with a road bent to Red Hook and a promise).
Who was the gift-giver, who pledged
what fortune for what prize?
Oh flats and steeples of Jersey City!
A country trembling immaculate
as a holy dream in the red-hanging hall
accursed in the eyes of a drunk.

Then we clapped aside the nacreous veils of luckless magic,
and passed into sight of the tall sails
of the hundred-masted city!
Shining like glass in the blazing lens of the sun.
This was my winnings, my castle, my island!
For all the never-at-home in the world
isn't there a city?
I slipped through its door like a thief.

·

They were sitting in the grass
and needed a wash.
But down on dirty knees
they stretched out the shivering taffeta,
and silver plastic on bamboo,
and then, let it go.
Away—away—up like smoke,
shaken and dazed like a big fierce bat-wing,
it bucked and rode
through the cold teething of the air,
it flew against a thunderhead over dark New Jersey,
touching the infinite verges of blue waste.
There, like a wavering neat star, it hung and blew,
until with a sudden wink,
it snapped in the hazy fetterings of space,
and the star twitched and dissolved,
flicked out like an eye.
One of them got to his feet,
his gold teeth gleaming,
his fingers making knots,
his face stared hungrily
up at the sky's empty square.
The wind boxed the collar about his ears.
He stretched and shuddered.
His friend dropped a pebble on his shoe
He cursed. At the roofless sky
he aimed a witless cuff.
They knelt and began to flatten out another.

                   •

Didn't I always want to be the man
walking in the rain,
coming down the dark street?
Didn't I want to be the rain?

Simmering in front of the bus barn,
slashing under car wheels like confetti,
and the lightning,
shearing aluminum foil
in giant notches
across the crumpling sky?
And the lights blooming in soft puddles,
and the wet policeman
flapped over by the swinging awning?
didn't I want to be myself,
naked in the window,
and the stinging of the thousand
flying waterneedles?
All of them—?

                    •

My daughter, eleven,
busy coming down from the bus, looked up
like a pop queen,
and all of a sudden, the omens turned bad,
the eggs gave in on their shells.
Her straw hat
was bent forward cap-like
to show me its raddled pony in red and blue
galloping across the straw-colored field
of the crown.
A porter pushed her happiness
ahead of him on the cart.
My heart made an audible knock.
What chatelaine of the world was this?
And whose prerogative was it
gave such a lady permission?
That she should bring it home to me,
and give it back like a game—
for what report could I make to her

of all those countries and persons
accounted mothers and fathers, designed to be trusted
and she was invested in,
that had failed?
How could I throw it far from her in the grass
like a dog to run for my humble news like a bone?

•

And of course there were fire sermons
to pay for it that year,
red, rising like flak
from the zone of the burnt cloud.
Silver cigars like dirigibles slithered,
cables flamed with messages from God.
Ultimatums rocketed up like light ladders,
brimming over and swimming down.
The wires of the rain fell, stretched out.
Telephone boxes and dead taxis
overflowed with burning zealous calls.
All mine, the whirling spatterdash of howling visual kisses!
Was it gone or to come, or was it only rumor,
the one warm moon
in the velvet waste without eyes,
the bottomless thicket
guarding the lost root?

•

Something was being divided up.
The last tags of the unfinished artist's life
hung from the truck like rags. And our painter friend,
with stupendous etudes set out under the moon
of ten-foot-high burnt-sienna banners,
and ten hundred blue-green chickens glued to the Bay Bridge,
trailed from the footboard.

That part had left us which was neat, tight, sensible,
deserted us and gone to mid-town.
What was left was divided, loaded, and hanging,
dangling off or fallen behind in the street
from the twisted body of the bent Mack,
drinking beer with the driver,
falling underneath on the cobbles with the drunks.

                •

This country of the sidewalk, consider it—
with its all-night songs of passion and candles,
a hunger whose name is murder the trees
beating out ballads of tenderness upon them,
leaning drunk to piss on them,
waiting for the cop cars to form in shining rings,
to press down the ritual stamp
like the street life of Corinth or Thebes,
ever doing that thing worth doing
which proffers its gift for a price.

                •

Ai! ai! for I am the Waltz of the Garbage,
whose battallions of sign bearers
beat their plaques into butterfly wings,
into zig-zags between cars.
There are shattered breakers of glass
like combers over the shores of my curbs.
The lights of fistulas hum in my cabs.
Faces of angry clowns toss grimacings
in smoking handfuls up through the windows
of clubs like bombs.
I discover the name of my city,
I christen it Mont Pele,
I duck head down in the mail-run of lava.

I toss my hot pennies
that sing to me of peace on the way.
Peace, that sounds like squadrons of wings of flies.
Insults change like suits of my clothes,
they shy up at the moon
and ricochet back from my foul-mouthed mothers.
The old woman who blows past
sadly looping in the wind, mourns,
as she wavers, "eheu! eheu!
what punishment for me!
What hounds me for all the hundred sins
that a thousand times
I steadfastly hated,
that I would never consider to do!"
While down in the subway caves
see, madmen are sitting.
Riding in electric excavations
calibrating bones,
scratching graffiti for signs of rain.
They master their horoscopes,
an eternal snow shovels down
whose cigarette papers flutter about like clouds
of the flowing pedestrian feet
that trudge and whirl to the caverns below.
Oh Waltz of the Garbage,
swaying in an air revolving with fires and screams,
your rage, like sunbeams, like music and come-ons,
is riddled like sieves with subliminal wishes of whores.
Oh Waltz of the Garbage,
Virulent dance where our lovers are dying,
we push them along through the gutters of going home,
bounce them through boutiques of dirty words
and past vintage years of the dregs of the sewers we ride.
We bestride them like horses of racing mud-black,

we speed them like mad kings to burial in stores,
we spin our sirens upside down,
backward we clang our bells.

　　　　•

When the rat climbs up our toilet from the drain,
he comes in up the sewer out of the stinking
tenements nearby shucked of their brick, like corn.
He glares at us with a wild incessant eye
that forces open the seat.
Busy, he starts out. Quickly we slam his door
and pour down salt, and ammonia, and chlorine,
on him with a wild clatter,
piling dead weights on the tank.
Later, we find him limp, a floating
foot-long seething kitten, and throw him out
with the trash. He bangs in the can,
but still, has become in some way, and partly, the winner.
For late at night, after the trucks are gone
and the stars run green, we hear him thump.
And run and sit on the bland white bowl of our lives
with its eye beset, like the heart of a curse,
and wonder what we've done to make him come
and scuttle about our dregs and skulk with our fear
in the under-basement draining our slums of thought.

　　　　•

It was twelve years in all,
before what was brought with us and what we provided
and what had been and what would be
became the ends of the same encountering choice.

It was a day of no reasons, that came when
the Hare Krishnas danced past on the way to the river,

under the sky like a blue temple bell,
in their happy mindless orange robes of smiles,
their barren heads and blue nose lobes.
They were chanting, westering down 72nd Street,
elaborating drums and bell sounds
riverward into the park.
I watched them go, and turning, came upon
Chase and Valda propped like tired dolls
in *La Crepe,* with under their elbows crumpled paper
and the crumbs of pancake.
Over their puppet-like trance a waitress presided
deeper in shadow than they were, wearing a grand baroque
blue Breton lace chemise and tall choker and hat,
and some bird croaked like a metal shriek,
re-making something else, from somewhere otherwise.

Was it the pattern of eaves,
the rounded cornices, buckles, loops, and anagrams
of the vast lace in stone of the Hotel Ansonia
across the street? That spirit of Paris
racing in 1895, that now totally
somnolent building dreaming of brains and verve,
as Stanford White saw it, drunk one morning on form?
Who was going to swallow a bullet walking his garden, soon,
for Evelyn Nesbitt, in the name of Harry K. Thaw.
—And these two friends—and my wife,
and the Breton girl and the Hare Krishnas, and the architect,
and the sun and the finger bells, came dropping
like links of recollection knitting a chain,
and sorted themselves with a foolish ticking sound
about the cornice of some all-circumferential
proud confetti-devising law. What an insane gift!
To sense a god-tremendous fearful arch of wands, jets,
circles, creepers, of three billion half-mad lives

intersecting, intertwined, that I was tight
anchored to, as well as the hateful enemy-lover of.
Tendrils grew to the ends of my fingers
and into the ground beyond
which was in itself (as I was also),
the holy city I looked for but could not find.
All wishes were leading to and from the root,
all things were secretly meeting each other
in assignations at dirty hotels.
Earth would be answered in the end,
however blind the reach and call.

Two Odes

After the fashion of Milton's L'Allegro *and* Il Penseroso

Reality Street

Reality is something like me carrying
the bicycle down the steps in the morning,
with a grip at the seat socket on the left
and the stem of the steering post on the right,
carefully placing my recently broken right foot
on the tattered step covering,
crazing open the doors with a little help
from my Puerto Rican neighbors.
"Gracias, gracias!" saying, especially if it's
the dark white-bearded one who shaves only once a week.
He will hold the beer can in the sack
with a far-away eye which seems to say
it is not I drinking this beer, opening the door
for this American with the suspiciously Spanish-looking wife.
Who rides a bicycle but a boy or a fool?
Help a fool is a kind of harmless custom.

The sidewalk is reality.
We have lost the last tree. The only one
to survive being pissed on and beaten.
And was getting to be a pretty good tree
in front of the shoe store, but obviously
rot had gotten in somewhere.
It failed in the wind last night,
and of course will not be replaced, except by
the beer cans and candy wrappers which seem to be
the true proofs of human occupation and human interest.
The bums in front of Garcia's are watching to see if Anselmo
will continue to sleep when the sun
comes over the roof of the Brittany building
and shines hard in his eyes.

Their interest isn't unkind.
Our bums take good care of one another around here.
I've seen two of them pick up a third
who had fallen off his egg crate in the street
and set him tenderly back up on end, teetering crazily,
and put his beer can again in his hand.

First, setting the bicycle off the curb,
I look back in the bus barn to be sure
nothing is coming out. With a quick hop and push
I set off against the traffic on the wrong side,
to the corner of 54th Street, then sweep
to the east, before them all, on that street, the one street
I know as I know my face or my kitchen table.
Reality! This is Reality Street—littered with
dog shit and broken auto parts, full of holes
and broken glass to protect a full block
of private cars of policemen in no-parking spots.
They know each other by their lodge signs.
Then the Youth Center, that used to be the night court.
I gather speed, sliding between the front bumpers
to the right, and the outside doors of cars to the left,
banking and spinning the pedals.
I've forgotten my broken foot, I'm flying!
Then I must wait to pass the paddy wagon,
they're loading up with girls—the wigged and raincoated haul
from last night's war sweep on Eighth Avenue.
The clean up! They're cleaning up the Avenue,
and professional fucking is being abolished again.
It will have to stand for whatever is being washed this week.
The girls are bored and angry,
they don't laugh when the cops joke
and the boys from the brick Greek church whistle.
The girls want to get on with their job,

of which this is a piece of the red tape.
I squeeze by and brake it at the corner.
Stopping, I rest, I beam at pedestrians,
It's 9 a.m.—Exuberant senseless beam—
these are not natives, but people going to work.
Four cops discuss departmental gossip.
They cross against the red light.
No one in this city obeys any law of any kind.
Cops less than anybody.

And then, I'm off again, going down
in the maelstrom of Reality Street. Everybody turns
at this place into 54th Street from Eighth Avenue.
Why? Are they going to the Municipal Parking Lot on the right?
Or to the unemployment office for waiters and dishwashers
on the left (a mysterious place full of crises
and explosions)? And there's the Bryant Hotel.
Alan Hovhaness lived there briefly last year.
I used to see his tall, hesitant, disjointed walk
mooning along thinking of distant extreme musical space.
"Hello Alan!" I'd yell. He'd turn and look as though
he'd never seen me before or anything before
and grin shyly. "Hello," he'd say.
Did he really know what was talking to him?
And now he's living in Seattle. That's reality.

Crossing Broadway is a sort of adventure.
This invincible instantaneous daredevil in me
is quite boiled down into a sort of egg-cup
of security and dutifulness,
but Broadway now, is something else, is always being excavated.
Don't you suppose the Mafia is holding a secret convention
down one of the holes, or digging a mysterious subway to Sicily?
They pave it again with asphalt and sand

as soft as chewing gum.
My bicycle rises up and rolls down
through hole after hole like waves,
honking bravely at all the pedestrians.
They look offended. Impudent motorless wheels!
They defer to cars, they respect trucks.
They've been converted to a religion of pure weight!

I skid to a stop at Seventh, and hurry across
through the taxi line for the airport trade
from the Hotel Americana. I park outside the crazy poster store.

Inside, I'm surrounded by Raquel Welch's breasts,
girls with steak quarterings on their rumps,
blonde nudes climbing cliffs, Nixon taking a dump,
calendars of Kamasutra positions, one per month,
four-foot-long inspirational zen poems on purple banners,
red fire-lighters a foot long.
I buy my paper, I fold it neatly behind my seat.
The clerk asks me about my foot. That's how
I'm fated to be remembered. The paper customer who broke his foot.
I walk the wheels to the corner
by half a dozen kegs of Schaeffer beer booming down
in the belly of the cellar of a bar.
I cast off past the Half Note and Jimmy Ryan's
to the Hilton, with its bus loads of Japanese tourists
craning their necks, casting about
at a crazily tilted perspective with sore ears
and sleep-confused eyes.
In these full, hurrying streets, what a difference!
Everyone is spruce, sure, full of purpose,
upholstered with money and sex in green,
knowing how to enjoy a breeze and walk hearty.
The flagpoles on the ABC, CBS, and Burlington Buildings,

the Warwick Hotel, flap with taut-natured snap.
This too is reality—or is it adventure?
I'm sailing in rash seas.
The light changes, four cabs crash through the red,
but we're wise to them—we wait,
and avoiding the dip in the street by the Athletic Club,
I nod at the doorman of the Dorset,
and now at the top of the rise, it's home-free,
I sail past the back garden and the trees
of the Modern Art Museum, avoid the driver-training car
of the Rhodes School, look up the skirts
of the girls with their books and their backs to the walk,
neatly slip past the back corner of a growling truck,
and up to the curb at the service drive.
There's a no-parking sign across the street
from the University Club. Really reality!

I put down my parking stand with a clang,
unlock the chain, unscrew the front half of my French bike,
it's beginning to rust from too much rain,
and I lay the front half beside the back,
chaining the two with a $22.50 hardened-steel five-pound chain.
This is reality too. Adventure with prudence.
Standing here, I think, I've made it once again
without re-breaking my foot.
—Look how they're watching me—. You actor!
A bicycle in two pieces! Such élan!
I stalk and limp to what will happen today.
Oh Fifth Avenue!

Fantasy Street

Feeling all at once imprisoned, I stalk for the door,
as I go, closing my coat up. Three gin-and-tonics—
no, I never should have allowed myself to have them.
But the hell with it.
Go!—get out!—get through the blunt glass
and off into the incalculable darkness.
Sure enough: as I burst out, there it is—
freedom! freedom! freedom!

It seems I am going to explode out of my skin,
to shout! By some miracle, I keep my silence.
The lights are amazing and flashing—Fifth Avenue!
The cold is like being struck by a soprano bell:
clear, fine, trembling, penetrating.
An Irish policeman outside Canada House supports the dusk
like a dark column or pedestal.
Shuffling his slow black feet he looks at me warily.
Am I too happy, too feverish? Might I be the camouflage
for our next I.R.A. bomber? Shaking with careless excess,
I push my bike across the south corner
towards 53rd Street, past St. Thomas Church.
This morning three young French artists
had drawn in chalk near the staircase Delacroix's
portrait of a peasant girl. It is almost half walked-off now,
ragged in the sodium-vapor light mixed with late sun,
but somehow still thumping with life, like an angry heart.
Suddenly I look up and have
stepped into a furious cockpit of battling cacophonous music.
A bagpiper on the church steps is squawling "Scotland the
                              Brave."
The clanless Highland vestment is Macspinningmill tartan.

"Help me get hame" says his sign. A boon he's been asking
                    six months.
There's talk he lives on East 76th Street with a Neapolitan
                    mother.
Tonight he will not have the street to himself.
Six yellow trucks across the way—
pasted prow to taffrail with signs—squall, screech,
swarmed about by crowds of little men in beards,
tieless shirts, black coats. The speakers jitter and skid,
throwing away horas between the Chassidic hymns.
It is the Lubavitcher bringing us messages from the Rebbe.
They inquire of every soul who passes,
"Are you Jewish?" They shout after us, "Wear phylacteries!
Observe dietary laws!" Shy little men with burning eyes,
they pop like skyrockets showering down on us with
flashing religious courage.
And straight ahead on the corner by the Tishman Building
the steel band won't give up: it hammers wildly, dexterously,
mellifluously, pouring out, over the already earthquake-torn
                    ears
of our intersection, "Yellow Bird."
It is battered to fragments by horas,
diced in the knives of the pipe chanters,
shot down over the crossway by up-to-date piety.
Enough! I run to the corner, almost throw the bike
ahead of me into the street,
fling myself on it like a demon.
A taxi klaxons by, coughing in my ear. Get out!
Fly! from the hell of this music! fly! fly!
At the end of such a day, give me a wonderful gift!
It is given. It's as though a door closes—
silence—all the madness trapped in the intersection
turns in upon itself. Only a hundred feet away
a single violinist scratches at Bach arpeggios

under the beggar's arcade at the back of the church,
uninterrupted, watched over by one serious girl.
And the Museum of Modern Art on the right gleams and
billows
like a wave of quiet illumination. Through the ground-floor
window
Marilyn Monroe's enormous lips poise to eat
a nameless art student looking somewhere else in a timid beret.
And now, up the left of the street advances that old beggar
who looks like Khrushchev. He bangs his vicious
steel cane upon the sidewalk like a shoe.
He pierces you with malevolent eyes, snarls.
"Hee!" he whines. "Hee!" jabbing his hand like a threat.
Now I'm gathering speed; everything begins to hurry into a blur,
the people in red, purple, yellow-green, violet
sew themselves along the quilt-strip of the sidewalk like checks.
My time of day! Excitement and events
bob in and out of windows like winking eyes!

Ahead, Sixth Avenue, and the hour,
and the kind of weather that makes me take a fierce breath.
The sky is full of clouds weighing hundreds of millions of tons,
overwhelming us like a wonderful painting.
Down southwest, vast new buildings glow with strange colors
like ice-colored blocks of honeycomb candy riddled with
yellow bees.
Now they fall over toward me under the weight
of enormous lilac and puce cotton cumuli streaked with smoke,
and salmon edges sliding along between upper surfaces
of hazy blue.
I put my hands up to protect my head.
I look out and nothing has moved—
and yet—don't I know absolutely everything has moved?

So it's all right. On! On! Across the street
fresh kitchen odors from the Hilton:
shrimp and cinnamon from this imitation New Orleans,
bay and thyme, garlic and parsley from that pretension of Paris,
and a smoky broiled steak from a mock Kansas City.
The kitchen ducts snuffle over the marquees like wet
                    commercial noses.
I glare at the animal doctor's office across the way.
My wife stood there the other day shouting at the nurse,
who would not ask her boss to look at Peter's gerbil.
Poor thing, with a paw swollen the size of a raisin,
all the local blood stopped by a tangled thread.
What kind of vicious snobbery chooses pet cats over pet mice?
On the second floor above is a sign,
"Stairway to the Stars Bellydance Studio."
I imagine them practicing their Phrygian birth dances,
palpitating from shaking diaphragm to the splay of the groin,
bent over backwards like some antique climax,
an ancient Busby Berkeley musical improvidence
with thousands of finger gongs tingle-ringing,
thousands of stars in galaxies ascending
out of silver quiverings up into the black empyrean.
Where are they now?
I am buffeted by the wind past the Americana Hotel.
I wave to the doorman of the old CBS building.
Proving his manhood, he sneers back.
Why is it I am slowly encroached upon by I don't know what?
The immense trenches of something going to happen
are about to swallow me.
It's after six, I go home like this every day, but still
my heart pounds like a riot policeman's feet, rapidly,
                    gloomily.
By the side of Roseland stands the old black man
I see here often slapping his tennis ball

off the back of the Dance Palace,
catching it again on his worn racquet through the weft of
                                    traffic.
His T-shirt says "Old Men Need Love Too."
He holds back his arm till I've passed by.
Thank you! I shake my head to drive away the fear
that relentlessly extends its wires.
Eighth Avenue at 6:15, and traffic like Ney's final
cavalry charge at Waterloo. Stupid, enormous, brutal,
meaningless—you can almost see the empty-headed marshal
whacking the brass guns with the furious butt of his sword.
And now I know something is happening. From across the
                                    boulevard
it catches my ear and eye.
Underneath bilious street lights some vast mob
is pouring out of the church in the center of the block,
each carrying a vespers candle.
And over them the sky has poured closer
as the buildings droop, against a half-darkness
of invisible sunset in front of which the clouds
dip and rise, stately, like great black-and-orange whales
spuming with anger.
Beyond the choir and the escort of police cars
I hear a flapping torn screaming,
a red banner of fire sirens and police cars
pasting together toward me across the extremities of sound.
What's happening? Is the Last Judgment arriving?
On a ragged spring evening when we know it's impossible
to put up with one more day of the old winter's ugliness?
No! No!—I get down, I hurry my bicycle
along past the army of illuminated penitents.
I drift beside them watching, presided over
by a sky full of brooding, distant, frightened wails.
Their soft faces over the candles are peaceful,

even earnestly fatuous, overborne with importance and duty.
"What we are doing"—they shine—"is so
very urgently necessary for this city—for us!"

But now I hurry past them
to the place where there are sounds of everything burning up
and thieves coming through all the windows.
Vast rivers of candles are turning north.
I wait, biting my lip as they pass by to the last baby.
I catapult my imagination
to the front of the Bodega Garcia,
where twenty-five of my neighbors wait quietly
standing on the sidewalk with beer cans.
It's cocktail hour.
Frantically I urge them, look up at the windows of my house!
Find out what's happening!
Is everyone there broken on the floor?
Is my kitchen crammed with policemen
looking at cut throats? Or are they—Is everyone gone?
Snatched away to Little Neck or Patchogue?
"Wait! Wait! Christ, don't go, even if you are dying,
wait for me! I'm coming, I want to go, too!"
My heart crowded with catastrophes, I vault across,
half running, half riding,
thick with foreboding and excitement,
pick up my bicycle and stumble up the stairs,
face full of tears.

POEMS FROM

Reality Street

1991

For Vladimir Mayakowsky

Words like express trains,
like galloping coffins,
are still being used like bites of sugar,
like noserags and pallid confections.
A sickness of the retreating national monastery
confuses language
with rest after selling,
with the piety of chapels
obliterating heads and mugging citizens.

Words are not escape, words are the thing!
Being used as a side tissue,
all the time they're the circus.
They stand ready for battle armed like a tank,
gusting flame.
See how the poet sidles up like a hairdresser?
Cunningly decorates earthsplitting rivers
so they look like the spit-curls of pages?

Book Burial

Among the Chou,
who ruled in China after the Shang and before the Ch'in,
there were an *Accomplished King* and a *Martial King:*
who came out of the land of Wei
in the far west.
They gave new laws.
But most of all there was among them
a marvelous exaggerated respect
for books and bronzes.

Scholars could do anything they liked!
And they carried everywhere tablets and brushes
suspended at the waist band
so they could write about it—
write down everything—
gossip—dirty jokes—grocery prices!
They were so proud of being able to say things
with their fingers! Oh, it was new!
And a serious consequential joy,
saying it ceremoniously,
saying it at all! With holy black calligraphy!
What pleasures!
They loved writing so much
they were buried with their books.
One king had himself interred with twenty
cartloads of classics on bamboo slivers.
That was a funeral fit
to make being buried worth thinking about!

I had always thought of being shot out of a cannon
into the mountains,
but no! This is the way I shall have it.

I'm resolved that if worse comes to worst
and I have to die,
well, I will insist on being buried with my books.
Now, first of all—in a rough cedar box
lined with broadsides, and funny poems.

Ugh! Spare me your bassinet linings
of pink artificial silk.
Spend the money on a good workable lamp.
If I should wake up, let me spend
the time reading.
Let my head lie on Saki,
let Yeats and Whitman and Cervantes,
Mark Twain and Chaucer, my pockmarked
pencil-scratched edition—lie somewhere about my fingers.
Emily Dickinson I shall have cast in bronze cartouches
to lie on my tongue. Put Hopkins on my chest.
He won't be heavy, he floats like hydrogen.

Thesaurus, wretched book!
Put that over my eyes.
Shakespeare, I will be all new-dressed
in your blue Yale edition.

If there should be room, throw in Su Tung Po,
Tu Fu, Dante, Joyce, and of course Basho and Issa.
That way I shall never get restless.
I shall never be tempted to come back
and twine about the chimney pots
of the still alive, jealous and

trying to make them uncomfortable.
Oh, I'll be quite happy, thank you,
for as long as you like.
What's best, when someday
they dig me up for my bronzes
to put my bones on exhibition
in a brightly lighted museum case,
I shall have come home
to a theatrical way of thinking,
and lie among minds moving about
in a place of learning and repose.

Nijinsky

Bending up the stairs,
dance case swung to my shoulder from the back,
I looked one flight above and saw Nijinsky
sitting on the steps—I swear—
his thighs wide-stretched and huge,
facing me with wild, high cheekbones, V-shaped chin,
clinging over me like an angry Scaramouch.

His eyes burned with a hollow light,
and stared in mine like a furious grievance brought to bay.
Contempt drew down the corners of his mouth,
made ploughed contours over the ridges of his eyes.
—you are too gross to speak of—he seemed to accuse
—old clot of fifty-eight,
desecrating my youthful art—.

"Exercise!" I stammered.
How could I make the ridiculous word compose itself?
I writhed in the contumely of his eyes
with their ghostly fire,
so the truth came hurtling out
like a series of *tours de reins*.
"I pickpocket a taste of it, that's all—for love."

His face cleared as though with a blast of light.
He grinned, fading,
and I swear, left a fleeting thought
as the stairs grew stairs again
and a tiny wind blew,
—Nothing excuses anything—nothing—
but passion's the most forgivable greed in a thief—.

Dog Dancing

Big Fred Carey hobbled over to me last night
in a dream, giving his heart-sworn thunderous grin,
reminding me how he'd once paid twenty a week
as I pumped gas from a Pure Oil station in Mountain Brook—
and how one time an old man parked his busted pickup
next, on the grass, some strange, lank kind of fellow,
whose beard was dirty, whose eye was witty,
whose truck was square in the back
closed off with a delicate netting of wire.

When he'd gotten a sack of day-old buns and rolls
from the bakeshop down the street,
he opened the veiled doors behind and called out a company
of trim little dogs like grasshopper children,
fox terriers and kindred mongrels on spindlylegs.
He watched them shake themselves,
then cranked his old victrola.
Hearing its stately scratches, the dogs began to dance.

What a strange sight, to see those dozen dogs
gravely turning about in slow pirouettes, hopping,
spinning in schottisches, somersaulting over their heads.
The old man stood there, watching,
slowly nodding, bidding them persevere
with squashed bits of stale bakery trash.
They silently waited with anxious fortitude
and gnawed crumbs in the wings like refugees.

On a tiny lady dog he strapped a pink skirt.
She treadled beneath the ruffles.
While the needle squeaked a bag-pipe wail,

she did a slow and mystic spin
with paws upraised and eyes in a heavenly transit,
turning and hopping, mincing her toes below.
When she'd done her turn, she took the old man's tambourine
between her teeth and grandly made the ring
of those who watched, and took their nickels and dimes.

I saw the thought fester in Big Fred's eyes,
that this old man, who should be safe somewhere,
sucking his pipe, reading the weather—
he and his dogs were out on the whim of the world.
"One morning he'll wake up dead," he said, whisking his hands.
"I mean, all right for him, he won't know better,
but what about the dogs?"
What was there I could say that he would believe,
and what did I know about the demands of art?

Artist

He groans at crooked construction,
at badly gauged shape,
as though they are dishonorings he must endure.

He hammers, sets, and braces
wood, earth, and water about him
into a junk carpentry of handfastness and hardihood.

Thinking of himself as merely keeping house,
he shames truth into "taking off its hat"
though Jewish, bald, or has a cold.
Arrogant, at gunpoint, must stop reality
fainting into gracefulness, or imitating fatigue,
must stubbornly arrange that what happens, naked,
shall fuck the future in public,
—whether or not either one likes it.

Then, having dug through rock to the heart of things,
bad-tempered, he kicks at life,
sniffs at what remains. What's it hiding?
Though hurt, he's happy to smash his toe.
At the bone is where life happens, is his faith.

So, heart-worn, crippled, fog-blind,
thoroughly skewed, if he still can't lie
in the name of kindness—or give it up—
he may crawl broken-limbed out to the end
of some frail tree, and once or twice
watch his patch of mud into earth that sings.

Skylark

(The Shelley Exhibition)

In the mirrored case our schoolfish faces
peer like guppies through the glass
at the darling sensual scrawl.
Big round actual tears
trickle and sluice down our wet nose-wings.
Oh liquid poet!
And we sob. (Didn't he weep in the Italian grass?)

But should the man arise from the glass case,
shuddering and sticking out his tongue,
to see all these becrutched ladies, schoolgirls
with a smirk, proper masters, glasses on the nose,
angry Ph.D.'s with popcorn bags, oxforded women,
arched like seals, sipping the wild wine of his pain,
which they will go out to wash down with a cup of tea—.

He'd wonder how the God who made the dizzy whirring
he sent round and round
made all us queer machines with grinding gears.
Wasn't he sent as a burning glass to cure our disease?
To melt our absurdities, along with his, into one?
But he has been, and does become, something else,
in time, and burns for us whatever we think, or are.
This minute, on the beach, on the white sand, if we wish,
as we add the wine, the earth, the salt,
and the oil, to his funeral pyre,
he will flare up against the Apennines of speech.

Inventory

It being late and quiet
and tonight
the planets not unfriendly,
I pick up the account book and write.

Item:
One bed here, cheerful,
split by two cracks
across the undertrussing,
propped on one side with casters,
spring busted.

Item:
Smells like laundry soap,
stiff sheets that rattle and crack
like silk.

Item:
Under the footboard below
an old cardboard suitbox
jammed to bulging
with eight Brobdingnagian books
of red-blue-green engravings
painted with six finished poems.

Item:
Note the enormous walk-away letters.

Item:
Up here about the head of the bed,
jostling like the people of a little city,
five hundred fiercely restless books.

Item:
To the left, my knee,
resting across my wife's knee.

Item:
She was crying a minute ago
across my arm and

Item:
Has gone to sleep,
lost with the ever encroaching thought
that she is moving along to be old,
—and it's true.

Item:
I'm getting there also,
and so is everything here moving along
spreading out from me in circles.
Away from here.
From the bed,
from the blue bedspread,
from the house, from the island around me,
from the sky spattered with planets.
Every one of them getting along,
every one of them belonging to me.
All of us lying here.

Item:
Not moving.

Item:
Moving along together.

Make Room

I want to finish redecorating,
be able to ask Death into my house,
show him the chairs,
the table I made myself,
crack him a walnut
(give him the good part),
introduce him to my children,
offer him a drink.
Which of us is the sly devil?
I'll say
I'm tired of keeping you hiding there
behind the door!
like a lackey.
Come out, come out!
Be proud of yourself.
No more sneaking,
walk in and give me a good short handshake!
Stay for lunch.
Consider yourself my friend.

Cats-Cradle

The land, pack on its back,
is up cap-a-pie in green, striding away whistling
rustling miles with a single smoke.
What's crippled and bent and caught unready
drips from its new boots, mossy spawn.

Roads weave their way like diamondbacks
hissing at counties of fervent basking—
blackbirds, a red army of shoulderboards,
quiver overhead shouting—

aspens breathless, turn coat over and over—
only an instant to cross the river,
(blue coat dripping stags)
it swims, running off field-mice and crickets.

Foolishness limps behind, scattering a flux
of wild seed secretly placed
here and there in the darkest groves
to steal up music.

The sky see-saws like a cats-cradle.
Over the hill, darkening, comes the sun to talk.
Ahead, sleep beckons, enormous shadows
booming both ways at once on the perilous throughway.

Velvet Gait

Night pulls up its cloak and belt,
breathes through its teeth the rain.
Lopside, velvet gait, its heels go tock
down roads swept dark of the moon.

Shadow on shadow, owls in its pockets,
sifting through trees, huffing its wing—
rests in a crack as the mockingbird plainsongs
through endless drift, change on change,
chimed for the ears of foxes.

Arms in tangles, flashing its black boots,
it weaves and writhes with rumbles of thunder,
thrashes a music through clearing and brake,
insolent as the trembling of hills.

It shakes Black Mountain deep to its roots,
breathes in life as it sighs out death.
Its name, it whispers, is whippoorwill wing.
Its empire is great,
vast as the chittering of bats.

Generation

I know my generation is to come,
waits to be thrust into life,
untied, unharried and unreduced,
foretold to be fantastic
like a two-headed eagle with fangs—.
Already in my sleep I babble about their coming.

The few who've got here so far,
eyes damp and lidded, get by
on lost luggage and wildflowers,
but—still living with one side bound
in the old flesh,
they flap like wind-starved sails.

Of course it's a double thought
of the warlock edge of the mind,
but whatever window I'm not at,
I sense those impossible brothers and sisters
rushing, hear their flyway and wing-thrust,
as they come bursting secretly through.

Up or Down

Bouncing from air-loom to air-loom like a
needle shuttle,
swimming in explosions, hopping with the sun,
caught on the fish-hook of light,
pulled up through cataracting visions,
coming around sea-beds on tangled tomorrows,
misconstrued yesterdays, multiplying nows,
I hear talk of old and getting old
and news of getting new,
and as though put on
like a coat by being born,
I am worn fashion to fashion
with the sheen of unwearying mythical cloth.
Tailor! tailor! fit me to light!
Sew new seams
in my ever-renewing rags.

Timehorse

How strange to mount this horse of time
that once set out, won't turn its mask,
and veers and bangs
about each coming back, to something new.

For instance, how you've circled home,
they give you such strange looks,
and the side of the house with its feathery shakes
is like looking through water.

Grandpa, late last week
recounting how he lost his coat,
hard as we listened,
he was only his voice,
sputtering whistles and creaks.

We say we trust in stars.
They're all that stays.
Cities break like waves.
And look, your friends that talked so much
have nothing to say but hands folded.

They threw us rice when we rode away,
now you yourself pull strangely on the reins.
Dusk falls on dusk like flickers of a film.
Money rolls in the streets.

Quarters and dimes, too fast to pick them up.
You snatch from the loving cup, as you were warned,
but tried as it passed both ways,
and the froth was dry before you could touch the rim.

Sum

This bed, these ears, this house, this city,
this world, these stars,
that stretch out five feet
to the tips of these fingers—
stretching me five quintillion light years
to the tips of them.
Lying here all colors, all pieces,
all hamsters, all magnets,
marble wears down someday to what I was.
Looking through eyes caught
looking over my shoulder,
clinging to carpets going away beneath my knees.
Every Sunday throwing myself out with the sweepings,
coming back in with the roaring of the trees.

The Fault Is

Some part of me keeps picketing the world
as though it knew of a better condition.
What have we for guide but what we're given,

or what we embroider about it
by terrified flight and mantic dreaming?
—that shriek in the night demanded what I thought.

—Was it a hare dangling by harsh talons,
or the grisly owl above, lordly grunting
and creaking, or the scream of the night-hawk,

clutching a more or less reconciled wood-mouse?
I saw no blood. Only feeling
hung there like a suspended question.

But I lay sweating as though mortally branded.
No way I could think of to be at fault,
neither hurt nor help, neither me nor mine,

But something had lumbered me with the job—
like it or not,
of settling the blame and the praise.

The Fanatical You

What to do with that creature,
thin and stubborn,
falling and hiding beneath
the coal heap of your conviction
who continues to believe in greatness?

How much time you have wasted
hunting him down with despair, this year, last year, next year
stretching the spotlight farther and farther
into his lair (it looks like the undercroft
of a mine of diamond carbon).
You spear where he hides, see his star-like eyes,
and that he wears nothing against you and the wet
in his fierce faith
but a silvery cloth.

You sweep the air with a lash of freezing wires,
he cries thinly.
You whisper "Come out!
Listen to facts for once."
But he roots farther out of the light
and lies under there starving,
nursing his knowledge like bread.
That he will outlive you.
That he will be right.

Being a Thief

The people of the forest, the Ruwenzori,
the Mountains of the Moon,
are stealthily proud of a skillful thief
who slips in and makes off
with eagle feather and cooking pot,
never awakening the dog.
Not for his being Lord Light-finger,
but for the perfection of his trade.
What country has struck a medal for the devoted whore?
Where is that tribe to which a dirty bum
is holy master if he is skilled in his art?

The world pickles what it does not approve,
acidulates the universe, (calling it keeping house)
to a moon like a pale homogeneous turd.
Bottles us up where its fantasies converge.
We yell, inside our jungle of dill
that we are that whore, that bum, that thief,
too knowing, too quick, too sensual of heart
to (either outwardly or inwardly) keep still.

Making Country

What a grand job that was.
Making country.
Two weeks
on the peaks and steeps of mountains,
and holes and runnels,
dressed at the tip
with feathers and copses.

Remembering, the method
with oceans
is fill them well to the brim
and line them with beaches
in neat verges.
Rake out the sand like a white unreeling.
Tick a picket of palm trees
here and there along the edges
like brushes.

Afterwards,
put the hours of a couple of days
to broadcasting deserts,
heaping the sand between the
wastes of boulders.

Walk off by moonlight, later,
scouring the channels of rivers,
scattering streams among hills
that glow in the dark
like silver lines on a map.

Hang it up overhead
(it will shine like a jewel)
and give it a twist.
Set it rotating.
Give it its own individual rate.
(That takes a most delicate hand.)

Stand off—
look at it there.
Violet, green, and coral,
spinning like a world.

Grandpa's Bedroom

Under the tin roof
of Grandpa's bedroom,
it rushes like a creek in a cave.
Waters bend their transparent elbows,
groping about the windows,
lightning splits the beech tree,
felled boughs bang the roof of my ear,
and clangorous air revolves with blue metal—
the carbide taste of the bolt.

Then, at once, the sheeted water stops,
the mountains move off in veils,
eaves and trees thin with dripping,
sing out of green grottos, "creek-bed,
cistern, frog-jump, water oak, sundown."
Vocables.

Overhead, the creaks and chirrs of blackbirds
gather in patchwork,
weave in and out their lines of flight from farms,
the sun, half-buried in vats of sorghum,
flutters thousands of winks through leaves,
scatters itself in throngs of butterfly legions.

Six o'clock comes rising
with its wringings of cicadas
squeezing the mists from the fields,
and night topples down,
smothering the sun at the pass.
As a dozen dogs vocalize and boom,
a whole new country of white slow fog
rises about the roads
spreading ice-blue snowbanks under the moon.

Buick

I am sitting
on the creek edge with my
feet in the water.
There is an oak log crossing the creek.
Off to the left, a path where animals run.
Possums and coons are running along it
through a forest where the creek
is running like a snake
through the middle of the trees.
The creek and the path and the forest
are running through me.

Among wild delphinium making thin blue-bell towers,
"Spring," says Sweet William.
He shines like pink, cheap jewelry
flung in the coarse grass everywhere.
Dogwood blazes in sheets of white crosses.
My father is digging at something
with his wild orchid pick.
An old Buick sits in the clearing
splendid with green plush seats,
and there is a garden at the edge of the forest.
Now, as I was in the forest,
I am becoming the garden.
Pick up the wet sack with the wild orchids.
Reach them high up into the back of the Buick.

Night Walk to a Country Theatre

Drop from the train's bottom step onto the grit,
turn out of the wind, ravel the hood of the parka tight.
It's gristly clear, the black night air fizzes with frost,
Venus and Jupiter sit near the moon like steps.
There's an old barge canal and water locks;
you cross on the steel plates, rubber soles clanging.
First a shallow skitter over frozen mud.
Then a steady booming of timed trudge
over the long bridge across the Connecticut,
frozen about the abutment islands.
They extend white claws.
Smoke steams from a chimney like a solid cloud.
Nobody knows you in any of the passing cars,
no obligation keeps you from climbing the rail,
dropping in the cold swirls of the water below.
Your breath comes fast, your spirit jumps
high above the iron network of girders.
On the far side, a strip-bar, evilly lighted, waits,
and long sidewalks of the tight-closed houses of strangers,
growling dogs, a rustle of distant throughway,
long lurching alone.
Then, through the darkness, rises up at last—
like a reward, as though you knew
this was how it should have been arranged—
warmth, singing, a cavern of people.
Your feet will have lost all feeling,
the joy will come flying.
It works every time.

To Betsy

Be rash and alive in your heart.
The worst fate is not having to die,
it's to be rolled—like sweat—
between the palms of somebody's weasly god.

There's a life's work
under the accountability of so many wonders,
coming to accept the simple truth
exploded all around us by the joy
of our skin and eyes.

Live at the Finisterre of feeling
if you want to think this world
is better than stone.

See, how it's your breath
puts the breath in the rock?
That you yourself
are the heat of the Spring and the fatal sun?
The more of you shows,
the less there is of you for them to hurt.

Soon, you will stir,
as though something had broken,
will awaken,
your own kiss will at last accept itself.
It will bruise your mouth
with the hateful miraculous passion.
It's our one gift.

Sweepings

Who's the Major Domo of the Principality of Peace?
How will I recognize his uniform and hat?
I keep walking, looking, peering under strange brims
hoping I can make friends with his face.

But there's no guidebook to this country.
Fly-specks and bird-droppings
have been mistaken for the map.
Where is the arsenal hiding, where it's made?

I look from my window each morning, waking,
hoping to spy the clerk
who throws out the sweepings from the work.

Coo Coo

Vivaldi, unable to sleep,
wrote a flute quartet.
Michelangelo, troubled with mosquitos,
painted God.
Carpenters cursed with kidney trouble
take out their hammers.
Bricklayers scour their trowels,
blacksmiths look for a horse,
lawyers lie in the shadow of a judge.
Others of us are boiled down to this thing,
this poem,
like scratching the Lord's Prayer on a tapioca bead.
Who can eat or wear or lie
in the shelter of a noise on paper
like a brown lichen?
Can it be mixed with anything to make colors?
A thousand of them couldn't raise you
ten paper piasters in the market.
The atmosphere is polluted with their puff.
We are sentenced to a form of expression
loathed by the Continental Congress,
forbidden by the fourteenth amendment.
Look, one of us goes past waving his wings like windmills.
the semaphore spells "love" as he is shot down—
(for an unauthorized flight).
But somebody, somewhere,
made money out of the crash.
The joiners of coffins
are considered to have more to do with maintaining life.
We are the coo-coos in the nest
surrounded by all the honest practical birds.

They say we are monsters,
we eat like ostriches
and kick everything native out,
then moult, flap on the flank of the abyss
yelling four letters!
The inevitable revolution
against coo-coos is on the way.
Soon they will recommend—look in the eggs—
otherwise how to make sure no more
are going to be born?
A bureaucracy will be appointed.
Decreed to be pigeons, coo-coos will
only be allowed to propagate in air-shafts,
eat the shit-seed of policemen's horses,
and anything shouting good news from the top of a clock
will be shot.
God, we grow strong!

Melt Out

Politics, you great glacier,
you have been going on for 10,000 years,
yet perhaps there is five feet of movement
in a hundred months.
Julius Caesar fell down a crack in 40 B.C.,
his body has just been sighted
emerging at the bottom of the pass,
frozen in a democratic attitude—
pebbles in his mouth.

Now Martin Luther King
steps in a crevice at the top of the pass.
Into what sort of world
is he going to come melting out, 2000 years from now?
And will 2000 years be enough
to freeze him naturally
in a non-violent smile?